Plank Cooking

The Essence of Natural Wood

Scott & Tiffany Haugen

Frank
Amato
PORTLAND

About The Authors

Scott & Tiffany Haugen live in Oregon's breathtaking McKenzie River Valley, east of Eugene. While their passion for writing is deeply shared, their true love lies in spending time with their family. Other cookbooks co-authored by the Haugens include *Cooking Salmon & Steelhead: From the Water to the Platter* and the upcoming *Smoking Salmon & Steelhead*.

Dedication

*To the two biggest miracles in our life, our sons
Braxton and Kazden.*

Published in 2004 by
Frank Amato Publications, Inc.
PO Box 82112 • Portland, Oregon 97282 • (503) 653-8108
Softbound ISBN: 1-57188-332-0 • Softbound UPC: 0-81127-00164-4
Photography by Scott Haugen
Book Design: Esther Poleo
Printed in Hong Kong

Introduction

The process of cooking food on cut wood dates back to Native American cultures on both the East and West coasts of North America. This style of cooking results in tender, juicy, delectable foods, ranging from meats to desserts. Today, plank cooking has been refined to meet the needs of modern-day appliances, such as grills, barbecues and ovens.

Woods that have been cut, planed, sanded and sometimes kiln-dried, present abundant opportunities in which food can be prepared. The result of cooking on a plank can be the best-tasting food ever to pass your lips.

Growing in popularity among restaurants and culinary institutes the world over, cooking on a plank infuses food with a rich, smokey essence. Rather than waiting for smoke-cured meats to enjoy the flavor natural woods have to offer, now, by cooking on a plank, the alluring taste is only minutes away.

The flavor of many foods, both savory and sweet, are dramatically accentuated when cooked on a plank. In addition, an appealing, ready-to-serve presentation can be attained directly from the grill or oven. To many people, the novelty of preparing food on a plank is especially enjoyable for both indoor and outdoor entertainment, no matter what the time of year.

This book contains many prized recipes and handling techniques unique to plank cooking. The comprehensive collection of recipes found in these pages are easy to master, while the ingredients are widely accessible.

Whether it's a nutty, mellow flavor you desire, or a robust woody taste you yearn for, your needs will be quenched with the recipes found in this book. You'll find that, due to the nature of cooking on wood, flavors may be even better the day after cooking, as the smoke and spices have had time to infuse the food. Freezing plank-cooked foods also preserves the special flavors created.

Once the basics of plank cooking are mastered, a whole new world of preparing food presents itself. When you discover the scrumptious flavors and exquisite textures that cooking on a plank has to offer, you'll be glad you learned these easy techniques.

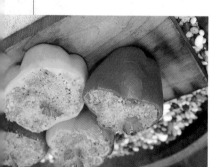
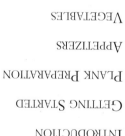

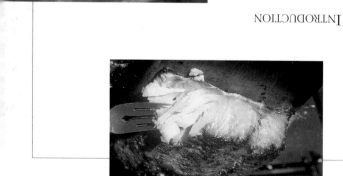

Contents

Planks, in raw form, can be cooked on as long as they have been properly dried.

WHAT TO LOOK FOR IN A PLANK

The more plank cooking you do, the more versed you'll become at targeting what tastes are most appealing. If you do a great deal of plank cooking, you may wish to explore outside the realm of the woods most commonly used; then again, you may be pleased with general woods like cedar or alder.

When cooking on a plank, avoid using resinous woods such as pine, fir, birch, juniper or poplar as these and other woods like them may contain volatile oils. If buying wood direct from a lumberyard or building supply store, be certain the woods have not been treated with any chemicals. You want either kiln or naturally dried hardwoods on which to cook.

If you have access to raw wood –- trees you can fall and split yourself — you'll find these natural wood "sections" make good planking material. Western red cedar, alder, maple and oak are some of the most commonly used woods in raw form, straight from the tree. The key to obtaining a good-quality raw cooking plank is

There are many types of woods on which food can be cooked, and all offer their own unique essence.

storing the split segments in a dry place where they can naturally cure without mold forming.

Due to convenience and safety purposes, most people elect to purchase prepackaged woods, ready to cook, from commercial producers of the product. The sportfishing company, Luhr-Jensen, produces a line of planks that are available from several retail stores throughout the Pacific Northwest. Planks can also be ordered direct from their customer service desk at 1-800-535-1711 or from www.luhrjensen.com.

The more plank-proficient you become, the more you'll want to experiment with different wood types. Deriving individual wood flavors can be accomplished by soaking planks in different liquids, but for a true change of taste, cooking on different species of wood is the best way to find variety. BBQWOOD.COM, based in Selah, Washington, offers one of the widest ranges of cooking planks in the country. These planks can be ordered in various lengths, widths and thicknesses, direct from their website.

When selecting a plank, make sure it will fit inside your grill prior to cooking.

In addition, BBQWOOD.COM features Sam's Smoker Pro, a unit that holds wood chips and fits inside your grill, serving as a smoke box to further infuse wood flavor. BBQWOOD.COM also produces a comprehensive supply of wood chips that can be used in the Sam's Smoker Pro, be it on the grill or in a smoker.

When obtaining planks, be sure the dimensions of the wood will fit inside your grill or oven, prior to cooking; if you have a way to cut larger planks to size, this is no concern. You'll also want to make sure that prior to placing it on the plank, the food will fit. The edges of planks tend to burn, so be certain the food can be situated on the plank with an inch or so to spare on all sides.

BBQWOOD.COM has one of the most comprehensive plank selections in the country, and can supply you with other wood-cooking products.

SOAKING & SEASONING PLANKS FOR COOKING

Prior to cooking with a plank, it must first be soaked. Soaking a plank serves several purposes, the main goal being to foster the absorption of fluids which ultimately keep food moist when cooking. This allows food to retain valued nutrients and results in a more distinctive taste. In addition to keeping foods from drying out, soaking a plank creates a more even cooking rate. This means food won't get overdone on the edges, while only partially cooked in the middle.

Fully submerging a plank in liquid is key to obtaining the best end product. Planks can be soaked for up to 24 hours.

Soaking a plank prior to cooking also reduces its burn rate when placed on the grill. The end result is a nice, woody smoke essence versus a harsh smoke flavor which can come from cooking on dry or charred wood. At the same time, soaking planks can prolong their life, even when used on a grill. If soaked and closely managed during the cooking process, some planks may be used repeatedly. Some of the harder woods, like oak, can be used many times if properly cared for. Planks used in the oven can last through dozens of cookings, as they are not exposed to direct flames.

While water is the most common liquid in which to soak a plank, fruit juices, vinegar, wine and other alcohols can also be used. Fully submerging a plank in these mediums imparts the light flavors of the liquids into the foods being cooked. If you wish to tone down the flavor of the liquids the planks are soaked in, mix them with water.

Soaking times for planks can range from one to 24 hours, with one hour being the minimum. Depending on the size and type of wood, as well as personal preference, soaking times can vary. Tight-grained, larger planks can soak longer than thin, more open-grained woods. The more experienced you become at plank cooking, the more familiar you'll be with soaking rates and how they apply to various wood types and flavors you wish to attain.

Once soaked, remove the plank and place it on the grill, cooking side down, at medium heat and allow it to dry out and preheat for five minutes; be careful not to let the plank catch fire. If cooking in the house, place plank in a 350° oven for 10 minutes. Once heated in the grill or oven, brush a light coating of olive oil onto the cooking side of the board. The oil will season the wood for cooking, keep food from sticking to the wood and help the food retain moisture and nutrients.

For additional flavor, rub a clove of garlic over both sides of the plank once it's

Once a plank has been preheated, brushing on olive oil prior to cooking will further season it.

For added smoke flavor, consider drilling holes in a plank. The larger the holes, and the more of them, the more intense the smoke flavor.

Partially drilling holes into the cooking side of a plank, then stuffing them with spices or pastes, can greatly enhance the flavor of food.

Narrow slats can be lined on the grill to accommodate either small meal portions or enough food for a dinner party.

been preheated. You can also lay a bed of fresh herbs, vegetables or fruits on the cooking side of the plank, then place the food to be cooked on top.

Planks, themselves, can also be modified to impart various flavors. Drilling holes through a plank transmits a deep smoke flavor into the food, especially when it's cooked on the grill. These holes, situated directly beneath the food, actually burn from the underside, through the middle. Planks that have been drilled need to be closely managed during the cooking process to control flare-ups. Such boards are typically used one time.

Drilling partial holes into planks and stuffing them with herbs or spices is another way to infuse unique, more robust flavors into the food. Drill the holes into the cooking side of the plank and pack them with your choice of ingredients. The holes can be filled with the desired spices or pastes after the plank has preheated, so as not to burn them or impart a bitter taste.

Narrow slats of wood also have a place in the plank-cooking world. Three- to four-inch-wide planks are ideal for cooking small foods, such as appetizers. In addition, several of these narrow slats can be placed side-by-side on the grill, whereby covering a large area. By leaving narrow, 1/8-inch gaps between the slats, the edges smolder and create a strong smokey flavor throughout. This can be efficient when cooking large quantities of meat.

Narrow planks, as well as regular sized planks that have been cut down in size, are great for dinner parties, with participants creating their own plank-cooked meals. Here, the meat of choice, be it a fish fillet or beef steak, can be dressed in herbs, spices, rubs or sauces by each

When cooking on a plank, never leave the area unattended.

individual. Each custom-created plank can be cooked simultaneously, and in the end, everyone can sit down and enjoy their special meal together.

WORDS OF CAUTION

When cooking on a plank, never leave the area unattended. When cooking on a grill, avoid repeatedly opening the cover as this can cause flare-ups and lost heat. When opening the grill,

Having a spray bottle on hand allows flare-ups to be kept under control.

A long-handled, metal spatula is ideal for transferring planks from the grill.

As soon as the food is done, remove the plank and douse with water. This will prevent fires and can preserve the life of the board.

Never place a smoldering plank on top of other wood. Here, the top plank was set atop a stack of dry planks, resulting in a potentially dangerous fire.

do not stand directly over the unit, as smoke and heat will escape. Be careful not to inhale smoke or allow it to billow into the eyes.

When cooking fatty foods, note their tendency to cause flare-ups in the bottom of the grill, even on the plank itself. With close monitoring during the cooking process, excessive flare-ups can be kept in check.

When the plank begins to smoke, check it to prevent undue flare-ups. Use a spray bottle filled with water to extinguish any flame on the plank. This approach not only prevents overcooking, it promotes a more robust flavor due to the increased smoke production.

If you're serving food directly off the plank, or moving the plank with the food still on it, from the grill into the kitchen, be certain to place it on a safe surface. The underside of the plank is extremely hot and can cause some surfaces to melt or catch fire. Having a large metal spatula with which to lift and transport the plank is a good idea and allows for easy placement onto a large plate or iron plank tray. Take care not to bring a burning or even a smoldering plank inside the house.

If removing food from the plank while it's on the grill, be sure to also remove the plank from the grill surface. It's good practice to immediately douse the hot plank in water, by either running it under an outside faucet or submerging it in a bucket of water. Not only can this process extend the life of the plank, allowing it to be cooked on repeatedly, but it prevents any possibility of fire dangers should the plank be haphazardly set aside.

A meat thermometer is a must-have device when plank cooking. Closely monitor internal temperature to avoid overcooking.

If your grilling unit does not have a built-in thermometer, a standing device placed on the plank provides an accurate reading.

A grilling unit featuring multiple control valves and vents allows you to accurately achieve the target temperature, no matter what the outside conditions may be like.

KNOW YOUR GRILL

Plank cooking is one of those undertakings that is best mastered through repeated practice. One of the key steps is getting to know your grill and how it performs. Whether you cook on a side-by-side or front-to-back burner grill, or cook on a briquette barbecue, it's critical to learn where the hotspots are. Some portions of the grill may burn hotter than others, which can greatly aid in the cooking of your food should you require more or less heat.

Grilling units featuring temperature-control devices are convenient, but not necessary. A standing temperature gauge works well, is inexpensive and can be placed directly on the plank when cooking to give the truest reading of the unit temperature. A meat thermometer is a must, especially when cooking large cuts of meat, such as a whole chicken, beef roast or pork loin.

When cooking over direct heat on the grill, that is, where the food is placed on the lowest rack, directly over the flame, use a low setting — if not the lowest setting possible. Cook with the lid closed so smoke completely engulfs the food to infuse flavor. The goal is to reach a level of heavy smoke in 15-20 minutes; doing so any sooner can result in uneven heating, likely burning the outer edges of the food. Once the plank begins to smoke, check often, spray bottle in hand, to extinguish any flames on the plank. This method promotes a strong smoke flavor.

When cooking over indirect heat on the grill, where food is placed away from the flame or in a hanging basket, use a medium heat setting. If using charcoal, pile the coals to one side and place plank opposite or elevated above the heat source. Cook with the lid closed, so the smoke surrounds the food to infuse flavor. Here, the plank should begin to smoke after 15-20 minutes. The plank should not catch fire when cooking over indirect heat. This method promotes a light smoke flavor, and takes longer to cook foods due to the lower overall internal temperature.

When grilling outside, weather conditions can be ever-changing, thus impacting cooking times. Outside temperature, humidity levels, even wind direction can impact the cooking rate of a grill. Cooking temperatures on the grill should range between 350-450 degrees. Knowing your grill and how it responds to varying climatic and seasonal conditions is important, and easy to learn with time.

PLANK COOKING IN THE OVEN

Plank cooking in the oven is another option. Though this approach is easy to maintain control over, it does not attain the concentrated smoke flavors achieved on an outdoor grill. Nonetheless, it is a very popular way of cooking, and it does impart a gentle woody essence into foods. One of the most appealing qualities to inside planking is the attractive aroma it introduces into the house.

Begin by preheating the oven and the presoaked plank, together, to 350°. Once the oven and plank have been preheated, oil the plank, place food on plank and put directly on oven rack. It's a good idea to position a foil-lined baking sheet on the rack below the plank to catch any drippings. Planks cooked in the oven can be used repeatedly. There are special, oven-only planks on the market, complete with internal adjustments rods that

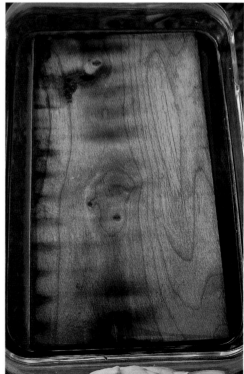

While cooking in the oven, planks can be kept partially submerged in liquid. This will promote a unique flavor in a moist environment.

As soon as a plank has been cooled, scrubbing the surface clean may prolong its life, allowing it to be used more than once.

When reusing planks, sanding the surface prior to the next cooking opens the grain, enhancing the flavor of the food.

Some planks, depending on species, thickness, and how they've been cured, can be cooked on more than one time. The new plank (left) is ready to go, and the plank at right is ready for a second round.

The 3/8" cedar plank (left) was used only one time, while the 1" slab of oak was cooked on 13 times before discarding.

allow warping to be controlled. These specialized oven planks are considerably thicker when compared to grilling-style planks and can be pricey, but the extended cooking opportunities they offer make them a good value.

Many foods, such as fish, seafood and vegetables, benefit from a moist cooking environment. It is easy to apply this technique when plank cooking in the oven. Simply place plank in a shallow ovenproof pan, partially submerging it in water or other liquids – do not let the liquids touch the food on the plank. Additional liquid may be added during the cooking to keep the plank moist and steaming.

When you're finished cooking on a plank on the grill, remove food and quickly cool the plank by submerging it or spraying it with water. This will preserve the plank, ensuring it doesn't continue to cook or smolder on the underside, or internally. If you wish to serve the food on the plank, spray the underside of the plank to cool it. Cleaning the plank is the final step, if you're looking to reuse it. Thoroughly wash it with warm water and mild dish soap. A one-part-bleach-to-nine-parts-water solution can also be used to clean and sterilize a plank. Scrub it to make sure all fat residues are removed and store the plank in a dry place, to prevent mold from forming.

When reusing a plank that has become slightly charred, go over the cooking side with a medium-grit abrasive paper. If you're reusing a plank that has been cooked on repeatedly in the oven, it's also a good idea to sand the surface, even though it may not seem to need it. Planks cooked in the oven can become laden with oils, masking the natural wood flavor. Sanding will recharge the plank, exposing fresh wood which allows for even cooking temperatures and better-tasting food. Be sure to soak the plank prior to each cooking session, and always preheat the plank which not only makes for more efficient cooking, but also sterilizes it.

WOOD TYPES

When it comes to selecting types of wood to cook on, choices and availability can vary from region to region, store to store, even with the changing seasons. Some people are content with using one or two wood types for cooking; others prefer having a half-dozen or more different woods on hand to diversify food flavors.

Following is a list of the most commonly used woods in plank cooking and the flavors they impart:

ALDER

One of the most common cooking woods in the Pacific Northwest, alder gives off a delicate smokey flavor while retaining a sweet quality. This is a widely preferred choice of wood when it comes to cooking poultry, fish, pork and vegetables.

APPLE

Many people prefer apple for the mild, yet somewhat complex flavor it creates. It yields a fruity smoke flavor with a hint of sweetness, making it a favorable wood for a wide range of foods.

CEDAR (WESTERN RED)

One of the most diverse, widely-used wood types for plank cooking. Western red cedar produces a deep yet lenient wood flavor. This aromatic wood is particularly good for cooking hearty, as well as culturally diverse foods.

CHERRY

Cherry is one that can give off a range of flavors. A tart, fruity flavor is created by this wood, with some varieties verging on the edge of sweetness. This is a good, all-around wood on which to cook.

HICKORY

A robust wood known for its strong smoke flavor. Hickory is one of the most common cooking woods in the South; the heavy flavoring makes it appealing for preparing pork, poultry, game birds and red meat.

MAPLE

A favorable smoke flavor is given off by this wood, while still retaining a sweet taste. It's one of the best all-around woods to cook on, as it nicely complements most foods.

OAK

A popular wood, oak produces an attractive smoke flavor that's great on a wide range of foods, including but not limited to fish, game, poultry and vegetables.

STEPS

1

Soak plank in water or suggested liquid, minimum 1 hour, maximum 24 hours.

2

Preheat plank on grill at medium heat 5 minutes, or in a 350° oven 10 minutes.

3

Brush a light coating of olive oil onto cooking side of board.

PLANK-COOKING OPTIONS

GRILL (direct heat)

Use the lowest setting on a gas grill or low charcoal heat. Place plank with food directly over the heat source. Cook with the lid closed so smoke surrounds the food and infuses it with flavor. Plank should reach heavy smoke in 15-20 minutes. When plank begins to smoke, check often — use spray bottle filled with water to extinguish any flame on the plank. This method promotes a heavy smoke flavor.

GRILL (indirect heat)

Use a medium setting on a gas grill. If using charcoal, pile coals to one side. Place plank opposite the heat source. Cook with lid closed so smoke surrounds food and infuses it with flavor. Plank should begin to smoke after 15-20 minutes. The plank should not catch fire using this method. Cooking time increases due to the lower temperature. This method promotes a light smoke flavor.

OVEN

Preheat oven and board to 350° or as stated in recipe. Place plank with food, directly on oven rack. Position a foil-lined baking sheet on the rack below the plank to catch any drippings. This method infuses a light smoke essence into food. Planks can be reused.

WARNING

When cooking, never leave planks unattended. Avoid repeatedly opening grill cover as this can cause flare-ups and lost heat. When opening grill, take caution not to inhale or stand in direct smoke.

Plank Preparation

Appetizers

Roasted Black Bean Dip

- 1 15-ounce can black beans
- 5-10 whole garlic cloves
- 1/2 medium onion, chopped
- 2 tablespoons ketchup
- 1 tablespoon red wine vinegar
- 1 teaspoon honey
- 1/4 teaspoon salt
- 1/8 teaspoon cumin
- 5-10 shakes of green Tabasco sauce
- 1 plank soaked in water
  (see page 15, "Plank Preparation")

Drain liquid from black beans. Gently mix beans, garlic and onion in an ovenproof baking dish. Place on prepared plank. Grill or bake at 350° 30 minutes, stirring occasionally to keep the beans from drying out. Cool beans completely. In a food processor or chopper, puree the roasted bean mixture. Add remaining ingredients and mix thoroughly. Serve with tortilla chips or drizzle into burritos or tacos. Keep any unused dip refrigerated.

PREFERRED WOOD: Alder, oak or maple. Use Simple Smoker (or smoke box with chips) to get a heavier smoke flavor.

RECIPE VARIATION: Add 1 cup chopped red bell pepper or 1 cup diced tomatoes to bean mixture.

SWEET BACON BITES

- 20 pitted prunes
- 20 whole, roasted, unsalted almonds
- 10 slices bacon
- 20 plain toothpicks
- 1 plank soaked in apple juice or water
  (see page 15, "Plank Preparation")

Soak toothpicks in water 1 hour or overnight. Stuff one almond into each prune. Cut uncooked bacon slices in half. Wrap bacon around prune and secure with toothpick. Place on prepared plank. Grill or bake in a 400° oven 20-25 minutes or until bacon is crisp. Serve hot.

PREFERRED WOOD: Alder, hickory or cedar.

RECIPE VARIATION: Substitute fried oysters for the prunes and almonds or whole water chestnuts marinated in soy sauce for the almonds (chestnuts will not fit into the prunes, place on top of the prune and wrap with bacon).

Appetizers

Baba Ghanouj

- 1 large eggplant
- 2 tablespoons canola oil
- 2 teaspoons tahini
- 1 tablespoon lemon juice
- 1 clove garlic, minced
- 1 tablespoon fresh parsley, chopped
- 1 tablespoon olive oil
- Salt and fresh-ground pepper to taste
- 1 plank soaked in cider vinegar or water
  (see page 15, "Plank Preparation")

Wash and dry eggplant, cut into 1/2" slices. Cut off and discard stem top. Generously brush both sides of the eggplant slices with canola oil. Place eggplant on prepared plank. Grill or bake in 350° oven 30-45 minutes or until soft. Cool eggplant completely and chop into cubes. In a food processor or chopper, puree the roasted eggplant with the remainning ingredients and mix thoroughly. Serve with pita bread or tortilla chips. Keep any unused dip refrigerated.

PREFERRED WOOD: Oak, apple or cedar. Use Simple Smoker, or smoke box with chips, to get a heavier smoke flavor.

RECIPE VARIATION: Substitute cilantro for parsley and/or substitute 1/2 tablespoon walnut oil and 1/2 tablespoon canola oil for the olive oil.

Appetizers

POLENTA ROUNDS

- 1 18-ounce tube prepared polenta
- 1 cup Pine Nut Roasted Tomatoes, page 44
- 2 tablespoons extra virgin olive oil
- Salt and pepper to taste
- Fresh basil, for garnish if desired
- 1 plank soaked in red wine or water
  (see page 15, "Plank Preparation")

Slice polenta into 1/3" rounds. Brush both sides of each round with olive oil. Sprinkle with salt and pepper. On a hot grill, sear grill marks into polenta rounds, approximately 30 seconds per side. Place 1 teaspoon roasted tomatoes on each polenta round and place on a prepared plank. Grill or bake in a 350° oven until heated throughout, 5-7 minutes. Serve warm with fresh basil.

PREFERRED WOOD: Alder, oak or maple.

RECIPE VARIATION: Additional toppings may include caramelized onions, roasted peppers or substitute Rosemary & Wine Roasted Tomatoes, page 43, for Pine Nut Roasted Tomatoes.

BRIE & CARAMELIZED ONIONS ■

- 1 medium onion
- 1/4 cup butter
- 1 large wedge or small round of brie cheese
- 1 plank soaked in water
  (see page 15, "Plank Preparation")

Slice onion into rings. Melt butter in a skillet on medium heat. Cook onions 20-30 minutes until tender, browned and caramelized. Cool completely. Cut top layer of skin off brie cheese. Place in ovenproof baking dish. Cover cheese with cooled onions. Place on prepared plank. Grill or bake at 400° 10-15 minutes or until cheese begins to melt and bubble. Serve warm with crackers or baguette.

PREFERRED WOOD: Alder, apple or cherry.

RECIPE VARIATION: Substitute Baked Brie en Croute for the brie cheese and place on top of the caramelized onions while planking. No dish is needed and the cheese can be served directly off the plank.

SPINACH-STUFFED MUSHROOMS

- 15-20 medium mushrooms
- 1/4 cup butter
- 1 tablespoon finely chopped onion
- 1 clove minced garlic
- 1/2 cup chopped spinach
- 1/3 cup bread crumbs
- 1/3 cup parmesan cheese
- 1/4 teaspoon Italian seasoning
- 1/4 teaspoon dried tarragon
- 1 plank soaked in white wine or water
  (see page 15, "Plank Preparation")

Clean mushrooms and discard stems, set aside. Melt butter in a medium saucepan on medium heat. Sauté onions until translucent, add garlic and lightly sauté. Add spinach, sautéing until wilted. Remove from heat, add bread crumbs, seasonings and parmesan cheese, mixing well. Generously fill mushroom caps with mix, packing it down.
Place mushrooms on prepared plank. Grill or bake at 375° 20-25 minutes or until mushrooms are tender and browned on top.

PREFERRED WOOD: Cedar, alder or oak.

RECIPE VARIATION: Stuff with Couscous Pesto, page 101.

Appetizers

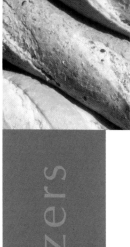

CHEESE BREAD

- 1 loaf French baguette
- 1/4 cup mayonnaise
- 1/4 cup parmesan cheese
- 1/4 cup medium or sharp cheddar cheese
- 2 cloves garlic, minced
- 2 green onions, thinly sliced
- 1 plank soaked in water
  (see page 15, "Plank Preparation")

Slice baguette into 1/2" rounds. Combine all remaining ingredients, reserving 1 tablespoon of sliced green onion for garnish if desired. Spread cheese topping evenly over slices of baguette. Place on prepared plank. Grill or bake at 400° 10 minutes or until browned, watch closely. Serve hot, garnish with remaining onions.

PREFERRED WOOD: Alder, maple or oak.

RECIPE VARIATION: Add 1/4 cup diced jalapeño chilies and omit green onions, or add chopped black olives to cheese mixture.

Appetizers

GRILLED HALLOUMI CHEESE

- 1 8.8-ounce package Halloumi cheese
- 1 teaspoon dried oregano
- 1 tablespoon extra virgin olive oil
- 1 plank soaked in water
  (see page 15, "Plank Preparation")

Slice cheese in 1/2" slices. Brush each side of the cheese slice with olive oil. On a hot grill, sear grill marks into cheese, 30 seconds on each side. Place on prepared plank, sprinkle with oregano. Grill 4-6 minutes or until lightly browned. Serve immediately.

PREFERRED WOOD: Cedar, maple or oak.

RECIPE VARIATION: Sprinkle fresh basil, parsley or chives over the cheese once it has been cooked. Kasseri cheese can be substituted for Halloumi cheese.

CREAM CHEESE CANAPÉS

- 2 loaves baguette bread
- 8 ounces cream cheese, at room temperature
- 1 egg, well beaten
- 1 2-ounce jar pimentos
- 1/2 5-ounce jar green olives
- 1 plank soaked in water
  (see page 15, "Plank Preparation")

Slice baguette bread into 1/2" rounds. In a small bowl whip softened cream cheese with beaten egg until thoroughly mixed. Cut green olives in half. Spread a teaspoon of cream cheese mixture on each slice of baguette. Top baguettes with 2-3 pimentos or 2 olive halves. Place canapés on a prepared plank. Grill or bake in a 400° oven 5 minutes or until golden brown. Serve hot right from the plank.

PREFERRED WOOD: Oak, alder or cedar.

RECIPE VARIATION: Use Kalamata olives, black olives or 1/2 teaspoon prepared pesto on top of the canapés.

Hot Artichoke Dip

- 2 6.5-ounce jars marinated artichoke hearts
- 3/4 cup mayonnaise
- 3/4 cup parmesan cheese
- 1 cup Monterey Jack cheese
- 1 6-ounce can black olives, sliced
- 1 4-ounce can fire-roasted mild green chilies, diced
- 1 plank soaked in water
  (see page 15, "Plank Preparation")

Mix all ingredients, reserving 1/4 cup parmesan cheese for the top of dip. Spread into an ovenproof dish and top with remaining parmesan cheese. Place dish on prepared plank. Grill or bake in a 400° oven for 15-20 minutes. Cool 5-10 minutes before serving.

PREFERRED WOOD: Alder, maple or oak.

RECIPE VARIATION: Substitute smoked or cooked flaked salmon for the artichoke hearts.

CURRIED MIXED NUTS

Appetizers

- 2 cups assorted nuts
  (almonds, hazelnuts, cashews, walnuts, pecans)
- 1/4 cup peanut oil
- 2 teaspoons curry
- 1 tablespoon Worcestershire sauce
- 1/8 teaspoon cayenne pepper
- 1 plank soaked in water
  (see page 15, "Plank Preparation")

Combine oil, curry, Worcestershire sauce and cayenne pepper in a skillet. Heat to a low boil. Remove from heat and add nuts. Coat nuts completely with oil mixture. Place on prepared plank. Grill or bake at 300° 10-15 minutes or until nuts are crunchy and dry. Cool completely before serving or storing in airtight container.

PREFERRED WOOD: Maple, alder or cedar.

RECIPE VARIATION: Substitute Cajun spice mix for the curry and omit cayenne pepper.

Pumpkin Seeds

- 2 cups pumpkin seeds, cleaned from pulp
- 1 tablespoon olive oil
- Salt to taste
- 1 plank soaked in water
  (see page 15, "Plank Preparation")

Toss pumpkin seeds with olive oil and salt. Make an edge for the plank using aluminum foil. Place seeds on prepared plank. Grill or bake at 375° 10-15 minutes or until lightly browned. Cool before eating.

PREFERRED WOOD: Alder, maple or oak.

CHILLED SALMON STICKS

■ 8 ounces plank-cooked salmon, chilled
■ 6 ounces mozzarella cheese
■ 1/2 cup basil leaves
■ 12 cherry or grape tomatoes
■ 24 decorative toothpicks
  (see page 15, "Plank Preparation")

Break salmon into 24 bite-sized chunks, taking care to remove any bones. Slice mozzarella cheese into bite-sized cubes. Cut or tear basil leaves to match size of the cheese. Slice tomatoes in half. Stack salmon, cheese, basil and tomato and secure with a decorative toothpick. Keep refrigerated until ready to serve.

PREFERRED WOOD: Alder, oak, maple

RECIPE VARIATION: Substitute plank-cooked ham or roasted bell peppers for the salmon.

Appetizers

Vegetables

Summer Vegetable Kebabs

Use any combination of the following vegetables:

- Onion
- Yellow squash
- Zucchini squash
- Red bell pepper
- Green bell pepper
- Yellow bell pepper
- Cherry tomatoes
- Pear tomatoes
- Mushrooms
- Olive oil
- Balsamic vinegar
- Metal or wooden skewers (soak wooden skewers overnight in water)
- 1 plank soaked in water (see page 15, "Plank Preparation")

Cut vegetables into cubes and toss lightly in equal parts olive oil and balsamic vinegar. Thread on skewers. Grill or bake in the oven at 350° 10-15 minutes or until vegetables reach desired crispness.

PREFERRED WOOD: Oak, alder or maple.

Vegetables

RED POTATOES WITH CORN

- 4 medium red potatoes
- 2 green onions, sliced
- 1 cup corn
- 1 teaspoon fresh thyme leaves
- Olive oil
- Salt and pepper to taste
- 1 plank soaked in water
  (see page 15, "Plank Preparation")

Wash and dry potatoes, thinly slice. Place potatoes on prepared plank, arranging slices slightly overlapping in parallel rows. Brush potatoes with olive oil. Sprinkle corn, sliced green onions and thyme over potatoes. Salt and pepper to taste. Cover with a foil tent to prevent charring. Grill or bake at 350° 35-40 minutes or until potatoes are tender. Garnish with additional green onion if desired.

PREFERRED WOOD: Alder, maple or cherry.

RECIPE VARIATION: Any variety of potato can be used successfully in this recipe. Potatoes can be partially baked in the oven or microwave to speed up cooking time on the plank.

Vegetables

TWICE-BAKED POTATOES

- 3 medium baking potatoes
- 1/4 cup butter
- 1/4 cup milk
- 1 cup cheddar cheese
- Salt and pepper to taste
- 2 tablespoons fresh chives
- 1 plank soaked in water
  (see page 15, "Plank Preparation")

Wash and dry baking potatoes. Pierce with fork in several places to allow steam to escape during cooking. Bake potatoes in an oven at 350° for 1 hour, or until soft. Remove from oven and cool slightly. Cut potatoes in half, lengthwise, and scoop out the inside leaving a thin shell. In a medium bowl, mash potatoes with milk and butter until fluffy. Add more milk if needed. Stir in cheese, salt and pepper to taste. Fill potato shells with mashed potato mixture. Place on prepared plank. Grill or bake at 375° 10-15 minutes. Garnish with fresh chives.

PREFERRED WOOD: Oak, alder or maple.

Vegetables

GRILLED GREEN TOMATOES

- 2-3 green tomatoes
- 2 tablespoons olive oil
- 1 teaspoon white wine vinegar
- 1 teaspoon Italian seasoning
- 1/4 teaspoon salt
- 2 tablespoons freshly grated parmesan cheese
- 1 plank soaked in water
  (see page 15, "Plank Preparation")

Slice tomatoes 1/4" thick. In a medium bowl, combine oil, vinegar and seasonings. Add tomato slices to oil and vinegar mixture marinating up to 1 hour. On a hot grill, sear tomatoes until grill marks appear. Place tomatoes on prepared plank arranging slices slightly overlapping, in parallel rows. Grill or bake at 375° 15-20 minutes. Sprinkle cheese on tomatoes during the last 5 minutes of cooking.

PREFERRED WOOD: Alder, maple or apple.

Vegetables

ACORN SQUASH

- 1 acorn squash
- 1/3 cup melted butter
- 1/3 cup brown sugar
- 1/2 teaspoon salt
- 3 tablespoons maple syrup
- 1 plank soaked in apple juice or water
  (see page 15, "Plank Preparation")

Wash and dry squash. Cut in half lengthwise, remove seeds and fibers. Place on a plate, cut side down. Microwave on full power 5-7 minutes. Cool squash long enough to handle and cut into 3/4" slices. Place squash on prepared plank arranging slices slightly overlapping, in one row. Mix butter, sugar, salt and syrup. Cover the top of the squash with the sugar mixture. Grill or bake at 350°-400° 25-30 minutes, or until squash is tender and topping is caramelized.

PREFERRED WOOD: Oak, alder or maple.

RECIPE VARIATION: Substitute any winter squash variety for the acorn squash. Omit brown sugar and maple syrup, replace with onions and garlic if desired.

Vegetables

COUSCOUS-STUFFED PEPPERS

- 4 large red, yellow, orange or green bell peppers
- 1 box quick-cooking couscous, any flavor
- 2 tablespoons olive oil
- 1 plank soaked in water
  (see page 15, "Plank Preparation")

Wash and dry peppers. Cut the tops off peppers and discard all seeds. Make couscous as instructed on package. Add additional spices or ingredients if desired. Fill peppers with stuffing taking care not to pack the mixture down. Arrange peppers on a prepared plank and drizzle olive oil over the peppers. Grill or bake at 350° 35-40 minutes or until peppers are tender.

PREFERRED WOOD: Alder, oak or maple.

RECIPE VARIATION: For a complete meal, add 1 cup cooked and seasoned ground beef, turkey or sausage to the couscous.

Vegetables

BELL PEPPER MEDLEY

- 1 green bell pepper
- 1 red bell pepper
- 1 yellow bell pepper
- 1 orange bell pepper
- 1/2 cup Italian dressing of choice
- 1 plank soaked in water
  (see page 15, "Plank Preparation")

Wash and dry peppers. Seed and cut into bite-sized pieces. Place peppers and Italian dressing in a plastic zipper bag, marinate 1-2 hours. Make an edge for the plank using aluminum foil. Place peppers on prepared plank. Grill or bake at 375° 15-20 minutes or until desired crispness.

PREFERRED WOOD: Oak, apple or alder.

RECIPE VARIATION: Mushrooms and onions can be added or used to replace some of the peppers.

Vegetables

CORN ON THE COB

- 3-5 ears of corn (or whatever fits on plank)
- Olive oil
- 1 plank soaked in water
  (see page 15, "Plank Preparation")

Soak unhusked corn 1-2 hours in water, fully submerged. Place unhusked corn on a prepared plank. Brush husks with olive oil. Grill or bake at 350° 25-35 minutes or until husks peel back easily and corn is tender. Remove husks and silk then serve.

PREFERRED WOOD: Alder, cedar or oak.

Vegetables

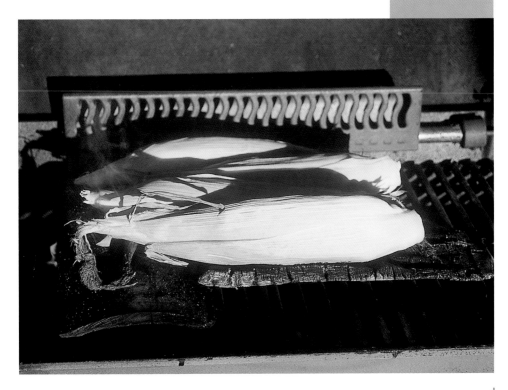

APPLE BAKED SWEET POTATOES

- 2-4 sweet potatoes
- 1 tablespoon canola oil
- 1 plank soaked in apple juice
  (see page 15, "Plank Preparation")

Wash and dry sweet potatoes. Pierce with fork in several places to allow steam to escape during cooking. Lightly brush potatoes with canola oil. Place potatoes on prepared plank. Grill or bake at 375° 45 minutes or until potatoes are soft.

PREFERRED WOOD: Apple, alder or oak.

RECIPE VARIATION: Substitute baking potatoes for the sweet potatoes and use water instead of apple juice to soak the plank.

Vegetables

ROSEMARY & WINE ROASTED TOMATOES

- 20-24 tomatoes
- 8 cloves garlic, cut in thirds
- 1 bunch green onions, coarsely chopped
- 1 1/2 tablespoons dried rosemary or
  2 teaspoons fresh rosemary
- 1/2 cup white wine
- 1/2 cup olive oil
- Salt and ground black pepper to taste
- 1 plank soaked in red wine, white wine or water
  (see page 15, "Plank Preparation")

Remove stems from tomatoes and drain. Stuff tomatoes with garlic and green onions. Place tomatoes upside down snugly in a 9"x11" casserole pan. In a small bowl, mix remaining ingredients. Pour over tomatoes. Place ovenproof dish on prepared plank. Grill or bake at 300° 2 hours or until tomatoes have browned and most of the liquid has evaporated. Serve as a side dish or puree for sauce.

PREFERRED WOOD: Oak, alder or apple.

RECIPE VARIATION: Any variety of tomato can be used, but the best results are achieved using paste tomatoes, such as Romas. Any variety of peppers complement this recipe. Additional herbs, such as tarragon, thyme and/or sage, make for a nice herbal infusion.

Vegetables

ROASTED TOMATOES WITH PINE NUTS

- 20-24 tomatoes
- 20-24 whole garlic cloves, peeled
- 1/2 cup pine nuts
- 1 tablespoon dried basil or 3 tablespoons fresh basil
- 2 teaspoons Italian seasoning
- 2 teaspoons garlic salt
- 1 tablespoon minced dried onions
- 1/2 cup olive oil
- 1 plank soaked in red wine or water
  (see page 15, "Plank Preparation")

Remove stems from tomatoes and drain. Stuff tomatoes with garlic cloves. Place tomatoes upside down snugly in a 9"x11" casserole pan. In a small bowl, mix remaining ingredients. Pour over tomatoes. Place ovenproof dish on prepared plank. Grill or bake at 300° 2 hours or until tomatoes have browned and most of the liquid has evaporated. Serve as a side or puree for sauce.

PREFERRED WOOD: Cedar, alder or hickory.

RECIPE VARIATION: Any variety of tomato can be used, but the best results are achieved using paste tomatoes, such as Romas. For a milder flavor substitute shallots for garlic cloves or stuff tomatoes with bell peppers.

Vegetables

MEXICAN ROASTED TOMATOES

- 20-24 tomatoes
- 1 medium onion, chopped
- 4 jalapeño peppers, seeded and halved
- 2 teaspoons oregano
- 1 teaspoon cumin
- 1 teaspoon chili powder
- 2 tablespoons minced garlic
- 2 tablespoons balsamic vinegar
- 2 teaspoons salt
- 1 teaspoon sugar
- 1/2 cup olive oil
- 1 plank soaked in vinegar or water
  (see page 15, "Plank Preparation")

Remove stems from tomatoes and drain. Stuff tomatoes with onions and jalapeño peppers. Place tomatoes upside down snugly in a 9"x11" casserole pan. In a small bowl, mix remaining ingredients. Pour over tomatoes. Place ovenproof dish on prepared plank. Grill or bake at 300° 2 hours or until tomatoes have browned and most of the liquid has evaporated. Serve as a side dish or puree for sauce.

PREFERRED WOOD: Alder, oak or cedar.

RECIPE VARIATION: Any variety of tomato can be used, but the best results are achieved using paste tomatoes, such as Romas. Any variety of chili peppers complement this recipe. For added spice, shake hot sauce over tomatoes after cooking.

Vegetables

PORTOBELLO MUSHROOMS

Vegetables

- 4-6 portobello mushrooms
- 1/4 cup extra virgin olive oil
- 1/2 teaspoon salt
- 1/2 teaspoon granulated onion
- 1/4 teaspoon granulated garlic
- 1/4 teaspoon white pepper
- 1/8 teaspoon paprika
- 1/2 cup mozzarella cheese, grated
- 1 plank soaked in white wine or water
  (see page 15, "Plank Preparation")

In a small bowl, mix all dry ingredients, set aside. Clean mushrooms with a damp towel or mushroom brush. Remove stems and scrape gills off mushrooms. Brush both sides of mushrooms with olive oil. Sprinkle seasoning over both sides. Place on a prepared plank. Grill or bake at 400° 10-15 minutes. Sprinkle with grated cheese.

PREFERRED WOOD: Alder, oak or maple.

RECIPE VARIATION: Serve on hamburger buns with all the fixings. Almost any cheese can be substituted for the mozzarella.

VEGETABLE SCRAMBLE

- 1 cup plank-cooked red potatoes, cubed
- 2/3 cup plank-cooked corn
- 2 tablespoons butter
- 4-6 eggs
- 1/4 teaspoon smoked paprika
- Salt and pepper to taste

In a medium bowl, beat eggs until frothy. Melt butter in a skillet on medium high heat. Sauté corn and potatoes until heated throughout. Push corn and potatoes to the side of the pan and scramble eggs to desired firmness. Add paprika, salt and pepper. Gently mix eggs with corn and potatoes before serving.

RECIPE VARIATION: Add planked bell peppers or substitute them for potatoes or corn.

Vegetables

Seafood

THAI RED CURRY PRAWNS

- 1 pound prawns, cleaned and deveined, leaving tails attached
- 1 tablespoon red curry paste
- 1 tablespoon peanut oil
- 1 tablespoon brown sugar
- 2/3 cup canned coconut milk
- 1 plank soaked in water
  (see page 15, "Plank Preparation")

Heat peanut oil in medium skillet on medium-high heat. Add red curry paste and brown sugar, stirring constantly until mixture bubbles. Reduce heat and slowly add coconut milk. Cook 5-6 minutes. Remove from heat and cool slightly. Toss prawns in curry sauce. Thread onto skewers and place on prepared plank. Grill or bake at 375° 5-6 minutes or until prawns are pink and slightly firm. Keep remaining curry sauce warm to serve over rice with the prawns.

PREFERRED WOOD: Alder, oak or maple.

RECIPE VARIATION: Substitute chicken or beef for the prawns, cooking time needs to be extended depending on which meat is used.

Seafood

Zesty Shrimp

- 1 pound shrimp, cleaned and deveined, leaving tails on
- 1 teaspoon smoked sweet paprika
- 1/2 teaspoon salt
- 1/2 teaspoon granulated onion
- 1/2 teaspoon dried oregano
- 1/2 teaspoon dried thyme
- 1/8-1/4 teaspoon cayenne pepper
- Ground black pepper to taste
- 2 tablespoons extra virgin olive oil
- 2-3 cloves garlic, minced
- Juice from 1 lime
- Metal or wooden skewers (soak wooden skewers overnight in water)
- 1 plank soaked in water, add 1 cup lemon or lime juice to water if desired
  (see page 15, "Plank Preparation")

In a small bowl, mix paprika, salt, granulated onion, oregano, thyme and cayenne pepper. Set aside. Pour oil into a shallow dish or pie pan. Arrange cleaned shrimp in one layer in the dish. Gently toss garlic with shrimp. Sprinkle on seasonings, including freshly-ground black pepper. Squeeze the juice from one lime over shrimp. Marinate, covered, up to 2 hours in the refrigerator. Turn shrimp at least 2 times while marinating. Thread 4-6 shrimp onto each skewer. Place on prepared plank. Grill or bake at 400° 5-7 minutes or until shrimp turn pink.

PREFERRED WOOD: Alder, apple or maple.

RECIPE VARIATION: Substitute prawns for shrimp. Prawns can be placed directly on prepared plank; skewers do not need to be used.

Seafood

LOBSTER TAILS WITH CILANTRO CITRUS BUTTER

- 4 lobster tails
- 4 tablespoons butter
- 1/4 teaspoon lemon zest
- 1/4 teaspoon lime zest
- 1/4 teaspoon orange zest
- 1 teaspoon fresh lemon juice
- 1 teaspoon fresh lime juice
- 1 teaspoon fresh orange juice
- 1/3 cup fresh cilantro, finely chopped
- Salt to taste
- 1 cup rock salt for plank
- 1 plank soaked in water
  (see page 15, "Plank Preparation")

Melt butter and mix with citrus zest and juice, salt to taste. Make four piles of rock salt on the plank. Balance lobster tails, backside down, on rock salt. Baste with butter mixture throughout cooking process. Grill or bake at 375° 15-25 minutes or until lobster is white and slightly firm. Discard salt. Serve with lemon, lime and orange wedges.

PREFERRED WOOD: Alder, apple or oak.

RECIPE VARIATION: Substitute garlic butter with parsley for the cilantro citrus butter.

SAFFRON BUTTERED BAY SCALLOPS

- 3/4 pound bay scallops
- 3 tablespoons melted butter
- 1/2 teaspoon saffron threads
- 1 teaspoon hot water
- Salt to taste
- Metal or wooden skewers (soak wooden skewers overnight in water)
- 1 plank soaked in water
  (see page 15, "Plank Preparation")

In a small bowl break up saffron threads and cover with hot water, let sit 15-20 minutes. Melt butter and add to saffron water. Thread scallops onto skewers. Baste with butter and place on prepared plank. Salt to taste. Grill or bake at 350° 5-7 minutes until white and slightly firm. Baste with butter 1-2 times throughout cooking process. Serve with lemon wedges and extra melted butter if desired.

PREFERRED WOOD: Alder, maple or oak.

RECIPE VARIATION: Substitute 1/2 teaspoon turmeric for saffron, omit hot water.

Seafood

GREEN SEA SCALLOPS

- 1 pound sea scallops
- 2 tablespoons extra virgin olive oil
- 6 cloves garlic
- 1 cup green onion, chopped
- 1 cup fresh parsley
- 1/2 teaspoon salt
- 1/2 teaspoon white pepper
- 2 tablespoons white wine
- 1 plank soaked in water
  (see page 15, "Plank Preparation")

Mix all ingredients, except scallops, in a food processor or mini-chopper. In a casserole dish, arrange scallops in one layer. Pour green sauce over scallops, turning to coat. Place scallops on prepared plank. Grill or bake at 375° 7-9 minutes or until white and slightly firm.

PREFERRED WOOD: Apple, cherry or alder.

RECIPE VARIATION: Substitute basil pesto or sundried tomato pesto for the green sauce.

Seafood

OYSTERS CROSTINI

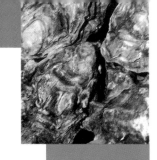

- 1 8-ounce jar small fresh oysters
- 4 tablespoons butter, softened
- 1 tablespoon lemon juice
- 1 French baguette
- Salt and freshly ground pepper to taste
- 1 plank soaked in water
  (see page 15, "Plank Preparation")

Cut bread into 1/4" to 1/2" slices. In a small bowl, combine butter and lemon juice. Spread butter onto each slice of bread. Top each slice of bread with one oyster. Salt and pepper to taste. Place on prepared plank. Grill or bake at 375° 5-7 minutes or until bread begins to brown. Garnish with fresh chives, if desired.

PREFERRED WOOD: Alder, oak or maple.

RECIPE VARIATION: Substitute smoked oysters for fresh oysters, omit salt.

Seafood

STUFFED STEAMER CLAMS

- 20 steamer clams, approximately 1 pound
- 1 tablespoon olive oil
- 1/2 cup pork sausage
- 1/2 cup celery, finely chopped
- 1/3 cup onion, finely chopped
- 1/2 red pepper, finely chopped
- 1/2 green pepper, finely chopped
- 1/4 cup fresh parsley
- 1 sprig fresh thyme or 1/2 teaspoon dry thyme
- 2 tablespoons clam water
- 1 tomato, diced
- 1/2 cup bread crumbs
- Lemon for garnish
- 1/2 cup coarse salt for plank
- 1 plank soaked in white wine or water
  (see page 15, "Plank Preparation")

Rinse clams well, discard any clams that are not clamped shut. Steam clams with lid tightly closed in approximately 1" water on medium heat for 15 minutes. Drain, reserving 2 tablespoons clam water. When clams are cool, carefully remove from shells and chop clam meat. In a large skillet, brown sausage on medium-high heat. Add olive oil, celery and onions and continue to sauté until onions are tender. Add peppers, clams and clam water, sautéing an additional 1-2 minutes. Remove mixture from heat and stir in

parsley, thyme, tomatoes and bread crumbs. Stuff each clam shell with the stuffing mixture. Sprinkle coarse salt about 1/4" deep on plank. On a prepared plank, balance shells atop layer of coarse salt. Grill or bake at 350° 8-10 minutes or until lightly browned. Discard salt. Serve with lemon wedges.

PREFERRED WOOD: Alder, apple or oak.

RECIPE VARIATION: Substitute fresh basil for parsley and Italian seasoning for thyme. Any size clams can be used for this recipe.

CREAMY CRAB

- 1 tablespoon butter
- 1/3 cup shallots, chopped
- 1 1/2 tablespoons flour
- 1 cup milk
- 1 tablespoon white wine
- 1/4 cup fresh parsley, chopped
- 1 cup crab meat, shelled
- 1/3 cup jack cheese
- 1/3 cup cheddar cheese
- Salt and pepper to taste
- 1 plank soaked in white wine or water
  (see page 15, "Plank Preparation")

Melt butter in a medium skillet. Add shallots, sauté on medium heat until soft. Stir in flour whisking until smooth. Slowly add milk, continue to whisk until sauce thickens. Add wine and mix thoroughly. Gently fold parsley and crab into skillet, salt and pepper to taste. Pour crab mixture into an ovenproof dish. Top with cheeses. Place dish on prepared plank. Grill or bake at 350° 15-20 minutes or until mixture begins to bubble and cheese browns. Serve with toast, rice or pasta.

PREFERRED WOOD: Apple, oak or maple.

RECIPE VARIATION: Double recipe for a larger group or substitute cooked salmon for the crab. This recipe can be made up to 12 hours in advance; double cooking time if previously refrigerated.

Seafood

Fish

CHERRY LEMON SALMON

- 1 fillet of salmon (3-6 servings)
- 2 tablespoons extra virgin olive oil
- Salt to taste
- Lemon pepper to taste
- 2 lemons, thinly sliced
- 1/2 cup fresh chives, finely chopped
- 1 cherry plank soaked in water
  (see page 15, "Plank Preparation")

Place salmon fillet, skin side down, on prepared plank. Brush fillet with olive oil. Salt and lemon pepper the fish to taste. Sprinkle chives over fillet. Place lemon wedges evenly over chive layer. Grill or bake at 350° 15-25 minutes or until fish is opaque and flakes in large chunks. Garnish with fresh sliced lemons if desired.

PREFERRED WOOD: Cherry, alder or maple.

RECIPE VARIATION: Substitute steelhead or halibut for salmon.

Fish

CHRISTMAS SALMON

- 2 5- to 7-pound salmon fillets
- 2 planks soaked in water
  (see page 15, "Plank Preparation")

SUNDRIED TOMATO PESTO

- 1 4-ounce jar or 1/2 cup sundried tomatoes, packed in oil
- 1/2 cup parmesan cheese
- 1/2 cup walnuts
- 1/3 cup fresh parsley
- 4 large fresh basil leaves
- 2 cloves garlic
- 2 tablespoons olive oil
- Salt and pepper to taste

Finely chop all ingredients in a food processor or mini-chopper.

BASIL PESTO

- 1 1/2 cups loosely packed, washed basil leaves
- 1 1/2 teaspoons chopped garlic (or 2 small cloves)
- 1/4 cup toasted pine nuts
- 1/2 cup grated parmesan cheese
- 1/4 cup olive oil
- Salt and pepper to taste

Finely chop basil in a food processor or mini-chopper.
Add remaining ingredients and blend to form a paste.

Lay salmon fillet, skin side down, on prepared plank. Spread pestos on fish in a striped fashion about every 3". Grill or bake at 350° 15-25 minutes or until fish is opaque and flakes in large chunks.

PREFERRED WOOD:
Alder, oak or maple.

RECIPE VARIATION: Both pestos in this recipe are great with any type of pasta. The recipe makes enough for two large fish fillets, but if making a smaller portion, the pestos refrigerate well up to one week or freeze for up to 6 months.

SMOKEY RUB ON ALDER

- 1 fillet of salmon or steelhead (3-6 servings)
- 1 alder plank soaked in water
  (see page 15, "Plank Preparation")

SMOKEY RUB

- 2 tablespoons brown sugar
- 2 teaspoons freshly ground black pepper
- 1 teaspoon onion powder
- 1 teaspoon garlic powder
- 1 teaspoon liquid smoke, optional
- 1 teaspoon salt

Thoroughly mix all rub ingredients in a shallow bowl. Lay fish fillet, skin side down, on prepared plank. Lightly score fish if thicker than 1". Gently but firmly rub ingredients into fish fillet. This rub can be sticky and needs to be slowly worked into the fish. If using a skinned fillet, rub mixture on both sides. Cook immediately or for a fuller flavor let the fillet marinate, covered, for up to 12 hours in the refrigerator. Grill or bake at 350° 15-25 minutes or until fish is opaque and flakes in large chunks. Garnish with fresh sliced lemons if desired.

PREFERRED WOOD: Alder, apple or oak.

RECIPE VARIATION: Substitute tuna or halibut for salmon or steelhead.

Fish

HONEY-LIME CEDAR SALMON

- 1 fillet salmon (3-6 servings)
- 1 tablespoon Worcestershire sauce
- 2 limes, thinly sliced
- 1 tablespoon honey
- 2 cloves garlic, minced
- 2 tablespoons softened butter
- 1 cedar plank soaked in water
  (see page 15, "Plank Preparation")

Marinate fillet in Worcestershire sauce for up to 1 hour. If the fillet is thicker than 1", inject with Worcestershire sauce and cook immediately. In a small bowl, mix honey, garlic and butter, set aside. Arrange slices from one lime on prepared plank. Place salmon fillet, skin side down, atop limes. Salt and pepper fish to taste. Spread butter mixture over fish. Place slices from the other lime atop the butter mixture. Grill or bake at 350° 15-25 minutes or until fish is opaque and flakes in large chunks. Garnish with fresh sliced limes if desired.

PREFERRED WOOD: Cedar, alder or oak

RECIPE VARIATION: Substitute steelhead for salmon.

STEELHEAD IN CORN HUSKS

- 6 corn husks
- 6 6-ounce skinned fillets of steelhead
- 1 teaspoon Adobo seasoning, or fish seasoning of choice
- 1/2 cup Miracle Whip salad dressing
- 1/3 cup onion, minced
- 1 plank soaked in water
  (see page 15, "Plank Preparation")

Remove corn and all silk from husk, keeping the bottom of the stalk attached to the husks. Rinse and dry husks. In a small bowl, mix Miracle Whip, onion and Adobo seasoning. Place one steelhead fillet in each corn husk. Evenly distribute the dressing over each of the fillets. Thoroughly enclose fish in the husk, tying the end with an extra husk. Grill or bake at 375° 10-12 minutes or until fish tests done. Serve in the husk.

PREFERRED WOOD: Alder, oak or maple.

RECIPE VARIATION: Substitute salmon or snapper for the steelhead.

Fish

Snapper With Creamed Vegetables

- 4 8-ounce snapper fillets
- 1 carrot, julienned
- 1 stalk celery, julienned
- 2 stalks asparagus, julienned
- 1/2 onion, thinly sliced
- 1 clove garlic, minced
- 2 tablespoons butter
- 1/2 cup heavy cream
- 1 lemon, thinly sliced
- 1 plank soaked in water
  (see page 15, "Plank Preparation")

Melt butter in medium skillet, add onions and sauté until translucent. Add remaining vegetables and continue sautéing 2 minutes. Add cream and heat throughout. Place thinly sliced lemons on a prepared plank. Place snapper fillet atop lemon layer. Pour creamed vegetables atop snapper and cover with foil, securing 1/2" under the edge of the plank. Grill or bake at 350° 15-25 minutes or until fish flakes in large chunks and is no longer opaque.

PREFERRED WOOD: Alder, oak or apple.

RECIPE VARIATION: Substitute raw julienned vegetables for the lemon layer. Red, green or yellow bell peppers add color to this dish. Pollack, sea bass or ling cod can be substituted for the snapper.

PESTO-TOPPED HALIBUT

- 4 6- to 8-ounce fillets of halibut
- 1 1/2 cups loosely packed, washed basil leaves
- 1 1/2 teaspoons chopped garlic (or 2 small cloves)
- 1/4 cup toasted pine nuts
- 1/2 cup grated parmesan cheese
- 1/4 cup olive oil
- Salt and pepper to taste
- 1 plank soaked in water (see page 15, "Plank Preparation")

Finely chop basil in a food processor or mini-chopper. Add remaining ingredients and blend to form a paste. Place halibut on prepared plank. Cover halibut with a thick layer of pesto. Grill or bake at 350° 15-20 minutes or until fish flakes in large chunks.

PREFERRED WOOD: Alder, maple or oak.

RECIPE VARIATION: Substitute cod or sea bass for halibut.

Fish

PROVINCIAL TUNA WITH CAPER BUTTER SAUCE

- 1 pound tuna steak
- 4 anchovy fillets, minced
- 2 tablespoons white wine
- 1 tablespoon extra virgin olive oil
- 10 gloves garlic, sliced
- 1 plank soaked in white wine or water
  (see page 15, "Plank Preparation")

CAPER BUTTER SAUCE

- 3 tablespoons unsalted butter
- 2 teaspoons fresh lemon juice
- 1 tablespoon capers

In a small bowl, mix minced anchovy fillets with wine and olive oil. Mash with a fork until well blended. Place tuna in a large zip-lock bag and add the above marinade. Marinate 1-2 hours. Heat grill to high heat, generously grease grill grates with olive oil. Sear both sides of tuna until grill marks appear, 1-2 minutes. Place sliced garlic on prepared plank. Place tuna atop garlic layer. Grill or bake at 400° 10-20 minutes, or until tuna reaches desired tenderness. While tuna is grilling, prepare Caper Butter Sauce by simply melting butter in a small skillet at medium-high heat. Once melted, add lemon juice and capers. Serve hot over tuna.

PREFERRED WOOD:
Alder, cedar or oak.

RECIPE VARIATION:
Substitute sturgeon or shark for tuna.

Miso-Glazed Shark

- 1 pound shark fillets
- 1 tablespoon clover honey
- 2 tablespoons white miso
- 2 tablespoons canola oil
- 1 tablespoon rice vinegar
- 1 tablespoon white wine
- 1 clove garlic, minced
- 1 plank soaked in white wine or water
  (see page 15, "Plank Preparation")

In a small bowl, mix honey, miso, oil, vinegar, white wine and garlic until thoroughly blended. Baste each side of shark with glaze and place on prepared plank. Grill or bake at 400° 15-25 minutes. Baste one or two times throughout the cooking process. Garnish with lemon if desired.

Preferred Wood: Oak, apple or maple.

Recipe Variation: Substitute sake for white wine. For a darker glaze, add 1 tablespoon light soy sauce. Striped bass or halibut can be substituted for shark.

Fish

CAJUN CATFISH

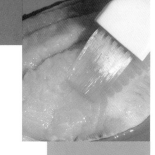

- 4 skinless catfish fillets
- 1/3 cup wheat or corn flake cereal
- 1 1/2 teaspoons salt
- 1 teaspoon hot smoked paprika
- 1 teaspoon garlic powder
- 1 teaspoon granulated onion
- 1 teaspoon thyme leaves, dried
- 1 teaspoon oregano leaves, dried
- 1/2 teaspoon white pepper
- 1/4 teaspoon cayenne pepper
- 1 tablespoon extra virgin olive oil
- 1 plank soaked in water
  (see page 15, "Plank Preparation")

Mix the dry ingredients in a food processor or mini-chopper. Brush catfish fillets with olive oil and coat them in the dry mixture. Place on prepared plank. Grill or bake at 375° 15 minutes or until fish is white and flakes in large chunks.

PREFERRED WOOD: Alder, maple or oak.

RECIPE VARIATION: Substitute any bass or walleye for catfish.

CRISPY-COATED BLUEGILL

Fish

- 15-20 skinless bluegill fillets (approximately 1/2 pound of meat)
- 2 tablespoons melted butter
- 1 tablespoon canola oil
- 2 cups Kix cereal
- 1/2 teaspoon garlic salt
- 1/4 teaspoon white pepper
- 1/8 teaspoon cayenne pepper, optional
- 1 plank soaked in water
  (see page 15, "Plank Preparation")

Melt 2 tablespoons butter and mix with 1 tablespoon canola oil in a small bowl. Measure 2 cups Kix cereal into a zip-lock bag. Seal bag and crush cereal into fine crumbs. Add garlic salt, white pepper and cayenne pepper to bag and mix well. Pour cereal mixture into a shallow baking dish. Wash fish fillets and gently pat dry. Dip each fish fillet into the oil and butter mixture and then into the cereal mixture, thoroughly coating each side. Place on prepared plank. Grill or bake at 400° 7-9 minutes or until golden brown.

PREFERRED WOOD: Alder, apple or cherry.

RECIPE VARIATION: Substitute crappie, smallmouth or largemouth bass for bluegill.

HERB-STUFFED TROUT

- 4 trout, cleaned with tail and head intact
- 1 bunch fresh parsley
- 1 bunch fresh dill or 1 tablespoon dry dill weed
- 1 bunch fresh cilantro
- 1 cup fresh basil leaves
- 3 tablespoons butter
- 1 lemon
- Salt and pepper to taste
- 1 plank soaked in white wine or water
  (see page 15, "Plank Preparation")

Lightly salt and pepper the outside and body cavity of fish. Cut lemon into four sections and squirt the juice into body cavity of each fish. Divide herbs equally among the fish, filling the body cavity of each fish. Set aside a portion of each herb to place atop the plank, and save a few sprigs of each herb to use as garnish after cooking. Divide herbs onto prepared planks. Lay trout atop bed of fresh herbs. Cover with a foil tent to prevent charring. Grill or bake at 375° 15-20 minutes per side.

PREFERRED WOOD:
Alder, oak or maple.

RECIPE VARIATION:
Substitute perch or steelhead for trout.

Fish

Beef

FLANK STEAK

Beef

- 2 pounds flank steak
- 2 tablespoons coarse salt
- 2 tablespoons extra virgin olive oil
- Fresh ground black pepper to taste
- 1 plank soaked in red wine or water
  (see page 15, "Plank Preparation")

Rinse steak and lightly score. Rub salt onto both sides of steak. Cover and chill for 2 hours. Rinse meat and pat dry. Brush with extra virgin olive oil. On a hot, well-greased grill, sear grill marks into steak, about 1 minute per side. Place on prepared plank. Pepper to taste. Grill or bake at 400° 5-10 minutes or to desired doneness.

PREFERRED WOOD: Alder, cedar or maple.

RECIPE VARIATION: For an Asian flavor, add 2 teaspoons Chinese 5-spice to the coarse salt.

PRIME RIB

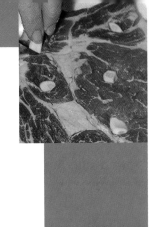

- 2-3 pounds prime rib
- 10-15 cloves garlic
- 4-6 fresh rosemary branches
- Salt and pepper to taste
- 1 plank soaked in water
  (see page 15, "Plank Preparation")

Rub desired amount of salt and pepper into each side of prime rib. Using a small sharp knife, pierce meat, inserting a clove of garlic into each incision. Place rosemary branches on prepared plank. Place prime rib atop rosemary. Cover with foil, tucking ends of foil 1/2" under plank to seal. Grill or bake at 325° 1 to 1 1/2 hours or until desired temperature is achieved. Uncover during the last 5-15 minutes of cooking, bringing plank to heavy smoke if desired. Rest meat 15-20 minutes before slicing. Temperature Notes: 125°: Rare; 135°: Medium Rare; 145°: Medium Well; 155°: Well Done. If cooking a prime rib that is over 6 pounds, allow a plank cooking time of 13-20 minutes per pound.

PREFERRED WOOD: Cedar, alder or oak.

RECIPE VARIATION: Cover prime rib with pesto sauce, see index (page 151) for recipe, omit rosemary.

Beef

SWEET SOY TENDERLOIN

- 3-4 beef tenderloin steaks
- 1/4 cup soy sauce
- 1/4 cup balsamic vinegar
- 1 tablespoon honey
- 1 tablespoon sesame oil
- 2 cloves garlic, minced
- 1 teaspoon red pepper flakes
- 1 plank soaked in vinegar or water
  (see page 15, "Plank Preparation")

Pierce tenderloin with a fork in several places. Place tenderloin in zip-lock bag. Add all other ingredients. Seal bag and mix by hand. Marinate in the refrigerator 3-12 hours. On a hot, well-greased grill, sear grill marks into steaks, about 1 minute per side. Place on prepared plank. Grill or bake at 400° 10-15 minutes or to desired doneness.

PREFERRED WOOD: Alder, cedar or maple.

RECIPE VARIATION: Any comparable cut of beef works well in this marinade.

Beef

PETITE SIRLOIN WITH MAPLE ONIONS

- 2 petite sirloin steaks
- 1 large onion
- 1/4 cup oil
- 2 tablespoons vinegar
- 2 tablespoons Worcestershire sauce
- 2 tablespoons real maple syrup
- 1 teaspoon salt
- 1/2 teaspoon black pepper
- 1 plank soaked in apple juice or water
  (see page 15, "Plank Preparation")

Thinly slice onion and place with steak in a large zip-lock bag. Add the oil, vinegar, Worcestershire, maple syrup, salt and pepper to bag. Seal bag and mix by hand. Marinate 6-12 hours in refrigerator. Place 1/3 of the marinated onions on prepared plank. On a hot grill, sear steaks for 2 minutes on each side or until desired grill marks appear. Place steaks on plank atop the onions and cover with remaining onions. Grill or bake at 400° 8-10 minutes or to desired doneness.

PREFERRED WOOD: Maple, cedar or alder.

RECIPE VARIATION: Add 2" of grated, fresh ginger and 2 cloves of minced garlic for an Asian flair.

STUFFED STEAK ROLL-UPS

- 2 pounds beef round tip steak
- 1 teaspoon salt
- 1 teaspoon white pepper
- 1 teaspoon dry mustard
- 1/2 pound sausage
- 2 tablespoons onion, minced
- 1 cup cooked collard greens, chopped
- 1 cup bread crumbs
- 1/2 cup parmesan cheese
- 2 teaspoons dry mustard
- 2 eggs, beaten
- Salt and pepper to taste
- Olive oil
- 1 plank soaked in water
  (see page 15, "Plank Preparation")

In a small bowl, mix salt, white pepper and dry mustard. Pound steaks to 1/4" and sprinkle both sides with salt mixture. In a large skillet, brown sausage. Add onion and sauté until soft. Remove from heat and slightly cool. Add remaining stuffing ingredients. Divide stuffing mixture equally among steaks. Roll up steaks, placing them skin side down on prepared plank. Lightly brush with olive oil. Grill or bake at 375° 20-25 minutes or to desired doneness. Slice before serving.

PREFERRED WOOD: Cedar, alder or oak.

RECIPE VARIATION: Substitute Pesto Couscous Stuffing for filling, page 101.

Beef

BETTER THAN BURGERS

- 1 pound ground beef
- 1 tablespoon Worcestershire sauce
- 1 tablespoon onion, minced
- 1 tablespoon ketchup
- 1 clove garlic, minced
- 1/2 teaspoon dry mustard
- 1/4 teaspoon fresh ground black pepper
- 1 plank soaked in water
  (see page 15, "Plank Preparation")

Mix all ingredients thoroughly. Shape beef mixture into patties. Place patties on prepared plank. Grill or bake at 375° 10-12 minutes or to desired doneness. If desired, sear grill marks into patties during the last few minutes of cooking.

PREFERRED WOOD: Hickory, cedar or alder.

RECIPE VARIATION: Substitute ground turkey for ground beef.

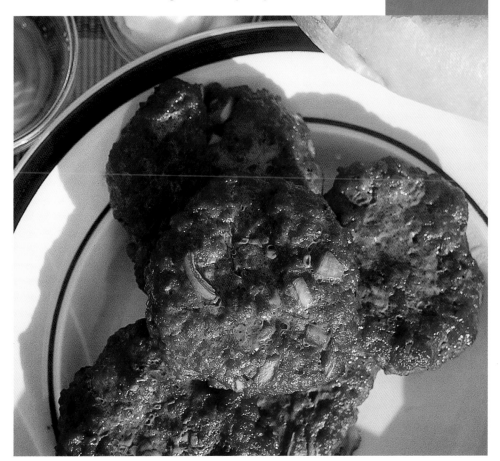

BEEF & PINEAPPLE KEBABS

MEATBALLS

- 1 pound ground beef
- 1/2 cup bread crumbs
- 1/2 teaspoon salt
- 1 teaspoon Worcestershire sauce
- 1/4 teaspoon fresh ground black pepper
- 2 tablespoons onion, minced
- 1/4 cup milk
- 1 egg
- 1/2 fresh pineapple, cut in chunks
- Metal or wooden skewers (soak wooden skewers overnight in water)
- 1 plank soaked in water
  (see page 15, "Plank Preparation")

In a large bowl, mix the above ingredients (excluding pineapple), until thoroughly blended. Shape into balls using approximately 1 tablespoon of meat mixture. Brown meatballs in a preheated skillet on medium-high heat, 8-10 minutes. Cool meatballs enough to handle. Thread meatballs on skewers, alternating with pineapple chunks. Place kebabs on prepared plank. Brush BBQ sauce on each meatball. Grill or bake at 375° 15-20 minutes or until meatballs are no longer pink. Baste with sauce several times during the cooking process.

BBQ SAUCE

- 1/4 cup ketchup
- 2 tablespoons red wine vinegar
- 1 tablespoon Worcestershire sauce
- 1 tablespoon honey
- 1/2 tablespoon Dijon mustard
- 1/4 teaspoon salt
- 3-4 dashes Tobasco sauce
- 1/4 teaspoon liquid hickory smoke (optional)

Mix the above ingredients thoroughly.

PREFERRED WOOD: Alder, oak or hickory.

RECIPE VARIATION: For a recipe shortcut, use prepared meatballs, your favorite prepared BBQ sauce and canned pineapple chunks.

PROTEIN-PACKED MINI MEAT LOAVES

- 1 pound lean ground beef
- 1/2 cup textured vegetable protein (TVP)
- 1/2 cup hot water
- 1 beef bouillon cube
- 2 eggs
- 1/2 cup cracker crumbs
- 1/2 cup diced tomatoes
- 1/2 cup cheddar cheese, cubed
- 1 tablespoon fresh parsley, chopped or 1 teaspoon dried parsley flakes
- 1/2 teaspoon onion powder
- 1/2 teaspoon garlic powder
- Ketchup for the top
- 1 plank soaked in water
  (see page 15, "Plank Preparation")

Dissolve beef bouillon in 1/2 cup hot water. Add TVP and set aside. Mix ground beef with the remaining ingredients. Stir in hydrated TVP and mix well. Shape meat loaf into desired serving sizes, greased mini-loaf pans work well. Place mini-loaves on prepared plank and top with desired amount of ketchup. Grill or bake at 350° 40-50 minutes.

PREFERRED WOOD: Cedar, alder or oak.

PASTRAMI WITH GREEN TOMATO RELISH

- 1-2 pounds beef pastrami
- 1 tablespoon olive oil
- 1 plank soaked in water
  (see page 15, "Plank Preparation")

Place pastrami on prepared plank. Brush with olive oil. Grill 20 minutes, bringing plank to heavy smoke. Heat throughout and serve with Green Tomato Relish.

PREFERRED WOOD: Alder, cedar or hickory.

GREEN TOMATO RELISH

- 4 green tomatoes, chopped
- 1 cup cabbage, shredded
- 1 green pepper, finely chopped
- 1 jalapeño pepper, seeded and finely chopped
- 1 teaspoon salt
- 2 teaspoons pickling spice (enclosed in mesh)
- 2/3 cup sugar
- 2/3 cup vinegar

Bring all ingredients to a boil in a large pot. Cool completely and place into jars. For best results "pickle" in the refrigerator one week before eating.

CHILI-CRUSTED ROAST BEEF

- 2 pound beef chuck roast
- 2 tablespoons red wine vinegar
- 4 dried California chilies
- 2 dried pasilla chilies
- 4 dried hot red chilies
- 10 cloves garlic
- 2 teaspoons ground oregano
- 1 teaspoon ground cumin
- 1 teaspoon black pepper
- 1/2 teaspoon allspice
- 1 4-ounce can diced green chilies
- Salt to taste
- 1 plank soaked in water
  (see page 15, "Plank Preparation")

Sprinkle roast with salt and vinegar, cover and refrigerate at least 2 hours, up to 12. Prepare chili seasoning by first discarding stems and seeds from the dried chilies. Break chilies into pieces, cover with 1/2 cup boiling water and let sit 20 minutes or until soft. In a blender or food chopper, combine drained chilies with the remaining ingredients until smooth. Drain meat and place in a large bowl. Cover meat with chile seasoning and let sit 30 minutes at room temperature. Place roast on a prepared plank, cover with foil, tucking ends of foil 1/2" under plank to seal. Grill or bake at 350° 1 1/4 to 1 3/4 hours or until meat reaches 140°-150° on a meat thermometer. Uncover during the last 15-20 minutes of cooking, bringing plank to heavy smoke if desired.

PREFERRED WOOD: Cedar, alder or oak.

RECIPE VARIATION: For leftovers, this recipe lends itself to many traditional Mexican dishes, such as chimichangas (page 84), tacos, burritos and enchiladas.

BEEF CHIMICHANGAS

- 1 pound cooked, shredded beef from Chili-Crusted Roast Beef
- 8-10 corn tortillas

GARNISH WITH THE FOLLOWING
- Salsa
- Sour cream
- Guacamole
- Jack cheese
- Lettuce, shredded
- Fresh cilantro
  (see page 15, "Plank Preparation")

Brush both sides of each tortilla with melted butter. Spoon shredded beef down center of tortilla. Roll tortilla and place in a well-greased baking dish seam side down. Bake in a 500° oven 10 minutes or until golden brown.

RECIPE VARIATION: Substitute leftover pork from Achiote Pork Roast, page 93.

Pork

SAGE PESTO PORK LOIN

Pork

- 2-pound pork loin
- 20 fresh sage leaves
- 4 cloves garlic
- Rind of 1 lemon
- 2 teaspoons salt
- 1 tablespoon olive oil
- 1 plank soaked in water
  (see page 15, "Plank Preparation")

In a food processor or chopper, thoroughly blend sage, garlic, lemon rind, salt and olive oil. Cover pork loin with the sage pesto and seal in a plastic zip-lock bag. Marinate 6 hours or overnight. Place seasoned pork loin on a prepared plank. Grill or bake at 350° 1 hour or until pork reaches an internal temperature of 160°.

PREFERRED WOOD: Hickory, alder or oak.

RECIPE VARIATION: Substitute Basil Pesto, page 61, or Sundried Tomato Pesto, page 61, for Sage Pesto.

SWEET & SOUR PORK

- 6 pork loin steaks or chops
- 1 tablespoon olive oil
- 1 1/2 tablespoons minced ginger root
- 3/4 cup sweet red pepper, finely chopped
- 1/4 cup red onions, finely chopped
- 1/4 cup crushed pineapple
- 2 tablespoons soy sauce
- 1/4 cup sugar
- 1/4 cup rice vinegar
- 1 tablespoon ketchup
- 1/3 cup cold water
- 1 tablespoon cornstarch
- 1 plank soaked in water
  (see page 15, "Plank Preparation")

Place oil in skillet on medium heat. Sauté minced ginger root 30-60 seconds. Add diced sweet red pepper and sauté until softened. Remove from heat. Mix soy sauce, sugar, vinegar, ketchup and chili sauce in a separate bowl. Return ginger and red peppers to medium heat and add above ingredients. Stir until sugar is dissolved. Mix cornstarch with cold water and slowly stir into sauce. Stir constantly as the sauce will thicken quickly. Once sauce is thick, remove from heat. Split loins or chops butterfly style. Stuff and top with sweet and sour sauce. Place on prepared plank. Grill or bake at 350° 35-40 minutes or until center is slightly pink.

PREFERRED WOOD:
Alder, hickory or oak.

RECIPE VARIATION:
To add heat, add 1 tablespoon hot red chili sauce to the sweet and sour sauce.

Pork

Sesame Ginger Pork With Miso Sauce

- 4 1" boneless pork loin chops
- 2 teaspoons sesame oil
- 3" fresh ginger, sliced
- 2 teaspoons minced garlic
- 1 1/2 teaspoons Chinese 5-spice
- 2 tablespoons soy sauce
- 1 tablespoon canola oil
- 1 plank soaked in sake or water
  (see page 15, "Plank Preparation")

Place pork loin chops in a zip-lock bag. Add sesame oil, ginger, garlic, spices, soy sauce and oil to the bag. Seal bag and mix by hand. Marinate in refrigerator 1-6 hours. Place pork steaks on prepared plank. Top with marinated ginger slices. Grill or bake at 350° 30-40 minutes or until center is slightly pink.

Miso Dipping Sauce

- 1 tablespoon clover honey
- 2 tablespoons white miso
- 2 tablespoons canola oil
- 1 tablespoon rice wine vinegar
- 1 tablespoon white wine
- 1 clove garlic, minced

Mix above ingredients thoroughly.

Preferred Wood: Alder, hickory or cedar.

Recipe Variation: Cube pork, marinate and thread onto presoaked skewers. Reduce cooking time by 10-15 minutes.

- 4 pork chops with bone
- 1/2 cup maple-flavored pork sausage
- 1 tablespoon butter
- 1/2 cup onion, chopped
- 1/2 apple, peeled and diced
- 1/2 cup cooked wild rice
- 1 slice wheat bread, cubed
- 1/4 teaspoon tarragon
- 1/4 teaspoon garlic salt
- 4 slices bacon, cut in half, for the top
- 1 plank soaked in water
  (see page 15, "Plank Preparation")

In a medium skillet, fry sausage until it begins to crumble. Add butter and chopped onion. Cook until sausage is completely done and onions are tender. Combine cooked sausage and onion with remaining ingredients. Butterfly pork chops toward the bone. Stuff chops evenly with stuffing mixture. Place on prepared plank. Lay bacon slices across the tops of the pork chops. Grill or bake at 350° 45-60 minutes depending on thickness of chop or until center is slightly pink.

PREFERRED WOOD: Maple, alder or hickory.

RECIPE VARIATION: Substitute prepared bread or cornbread stuffing for wild rice.

Pork

SAUCY SPARERIBS

- 1 rack pork spareribs
- 1 plank soaked in apple juice or water
  (see page 15, "Plank Preparation")

SAUCE

- 1/4 cup Worcestershire sauce
- 1/4 cup cider vinegar
- 1/3 cup brown sugar
- 1/3 cup ketchup
- 1 teaspoon salt
- 1/2 teaspoon ground black pepper
- 1 green pepper, chopped
- 1 onion, chopped
- 3 cloves garlic
- 1 can pineapple with juice
- Dash of hot pepper sauce, if desired

In a medium saucepan, mix all above sauce ingredients. Bring to a light boil and reduce heat. Simmer 10-20 minutes on low heat, cool completely. Clean any loose fat and membrane off pork ribs. Place ribs on a large sheet of foil and cover with 1/2 of the cooled sauce. Marinate ribs 3-5 hours at room temperature. Place foil-covered ribs on the grill for 45 minutes. Remove foil, place ribs on a prepared plank, basting frequently with the remainder of the sauce. Cook an additional 30 minutes or until tender.

PREFERRED WOOD: Alder, cedar or hickory.

Pork

ACHIOTE PORK ROAST

- 1 3-pound boneless pork shoulder
- 2 tablespoons annatto seeds
- 1 tablespoon warm water
- 1 teaspoon cumin seeds
- 1 teaspoon ground oregano
- 1 teaspoon allspice
- 1 teaspoon salt
- 4-6 garlic cloves
- 3 tablespoons lime juice
- 1/2 teaspoon lime zest
- 1 plank soaked in water
  (see page 15, "Plank Preparation")

Soak annatto seeds overnight in 1 tablespoon warm water. In a food chopper or blender, thoroughly mix soaked annatto seeds, spices, garlic, lime juice and zest. Deeply pierce pork shoulder with a fork in several places. Place pork in a zip-lock bag. Add achiote mixture. Seal bag and mix by hand. Refrigerate 12-24 hours. Place roast on a prepared plank, cover with foil, tucking ends of foil 1/2" under plank to seal. Grill or bake at 350° 1 1/2 to 2 hours or until internal temperature reaches 160°. Uncover during the last 15-20 minutes of cooking and bring plank to heavy smoke if desired. Serve with beans, rice and warm tortillas if desired.

PREFERRED WOOD:
Hickory, alder or oak.

RECIPE VARIATION:
For leftovers, this recipe lends itself to many traditional Mexican dishes such as burritos (page 94), tacos, chimichangas and enchiladas.

Pork

PORK BURRITOS

- 1 pound cooked, shredded pork from Achiote Pork Roast
- 4-6 large flour tortillas
- 1 15-ounce can black or pinto beans
- 2 cups Jack cheese, shredded
- 1/2 cup fresh cilantro leaves

GARNISH WITH THE FOLLOWING

- Salsa
- Sour cream
- Guacamole
- Lettuce, shredded
- Jack cheese

Wrap tortillas in foil and heat in a 350° oven for 10-15 minutes. In a large sauce pan, mix shredded pork and beans on medium heat until warmed throughout. Spoon shredded pork filling down the center of each tortilla, sprinkle with cheese and cilantro. Fold sides in and roll up, placing seam side down on serving platter.

BRATWURST

- 1 pound bratwurst
- Grill Rub, page 119
- 1 plank soaked in beer or water
  (see page 15, "Plank Preparation")

Work grill rub into all sides of the bratwurst. Let sit at room temperature 10-20 minutes. Sear all sides of bratwurst on high heat. Place on prepared plank. Grill or bake at 375° 25-30 minutes. Serve on a hoagie roll with all the fixings.

PREFERRED WOOD: Alder, oak or hickory.

Pork

DOUBLE-SMOKED CITRUS HAM

- 1 3- to 5-pound fully-cooked picnic ham
- 1 cup brown sugar
- Juice from 1 lime
- 1 can crushed pineapple
- 1 plank soaked in orange juice or water
  (see page 15, "Plank Preparation")

Score ham and rub with brown sugar, let sit 10-15 minutes. Drain pineapple juice, replacing with lime juice. Coat ham with pineapple and lime mixture. Place on prepared plank. Cover ham loosely with foil. Grill or bake at 350° 1 1/2 to 2 hours or until ham reaches an internal temperature of 110°.

PREFERRED WOOD: Alder, hickory or maple.

Pork

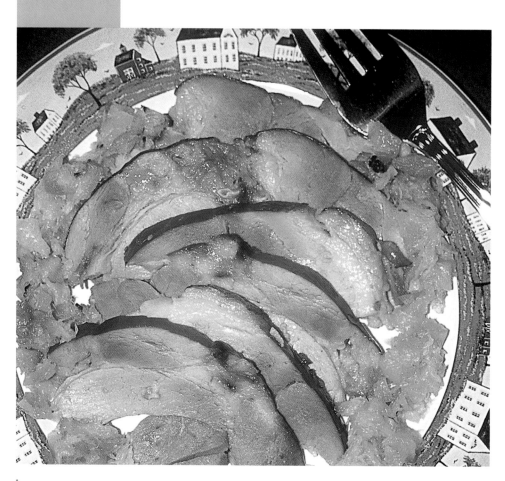

PORK & PEPPER STIR FRY

- 2 cups cooked Sage Pesto Pork Loin, cubed
- 1 tablespoon canola oil
- 1/2 onion, chopped
- 1 yellow bell pepper, chopped
- 1 red bell pepper, chopped
- 1 medium zucchini, halved and sliced
- 2 teaspoons soy sauce
- Salt and pepper to taste

In a large skillet, heat oil on medium-high heat. Add onion and stir-fry until tender. Add peppers and zucchini, sauté an additional 5 minutes. Add cooked pork and soy sauce, heating to desired temperature. Salt and pepper to taste. Serve with rice or soba noodles.

PREFERRED WOOD: Alder, oak or maple.

RECIPE VARIATION: Substitute Sesame Ginger Pork Loin, page 90, and bamboo shoots, bean sprouts and water chestnuts for the peppers and zucchini.

Pork

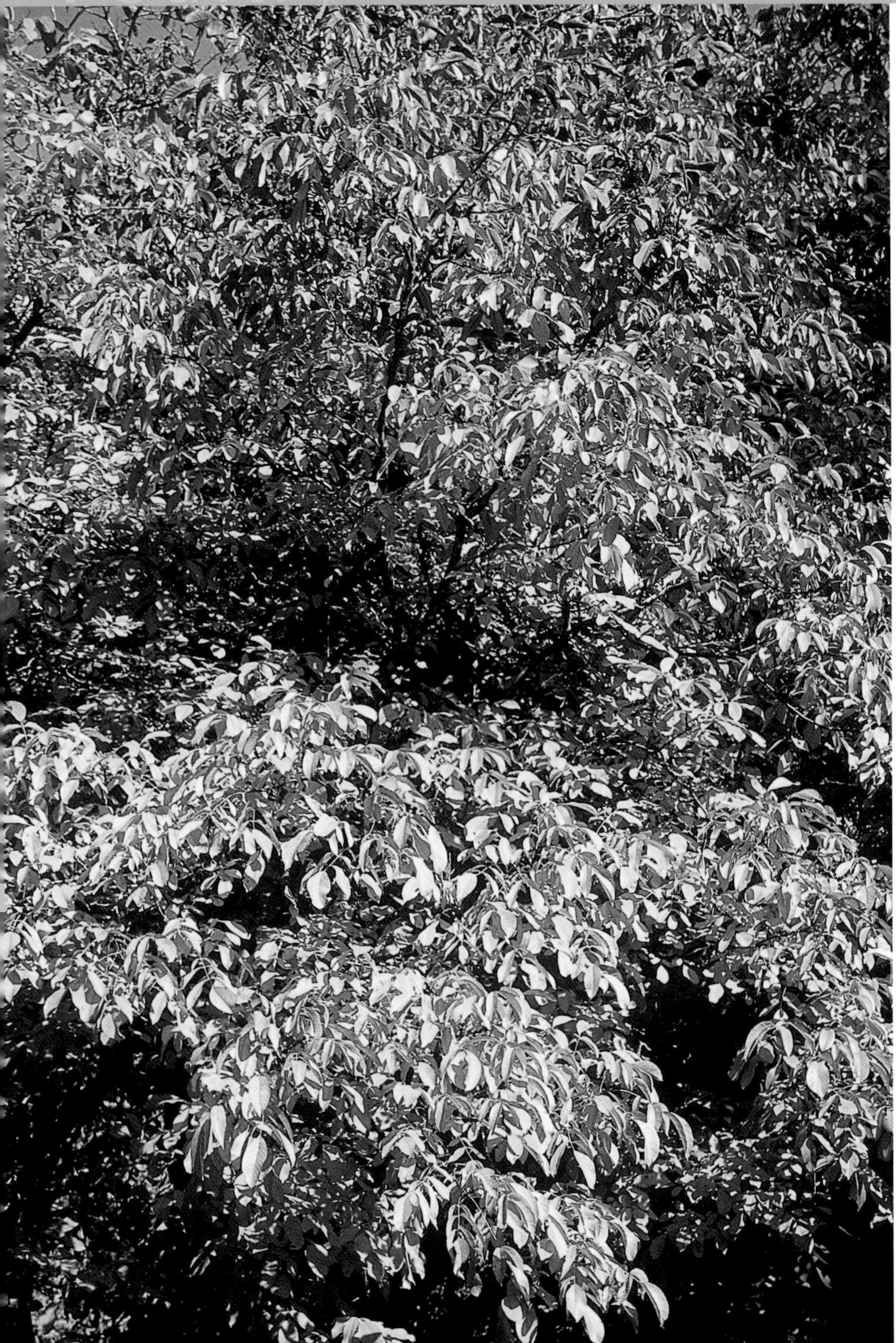

Poultry

HERB ROASTED CHICKEN

- 1/2 whole chicken
- 3 tablespoons olive oil
- 1 tablespoon fresh rosemary
- 1/2 tablespoon fresh thyme
- Juice of 1/2 lemon
- Salt and pepper to taste
- 1 onion, sliced
- 1 lemon, sliced
- 1 plank soaked in white wine or water
  (see page 15, "Plank Preparation")

Place chicken in a medium bowl. Add olive oil, herbs, lemon juice, salt and pepper. Marinate chicken in the refrigerator, turning occasionally, from 1-6 hours. Place sliced onions and lemons on a prepared plank. Flatten chicken, skin side up, atop onion and lemon layer. Grill or bake at 350° 50-60 minutes or until juices run clear.

PREFERRED WOOD: Alder, oak or maple.

RECIPE VARIATION: Any combination of fresh or dried herbs can be used in this recipe. For a quick meal, simply marinate chicken in prepared Italian dressing.

Poultry

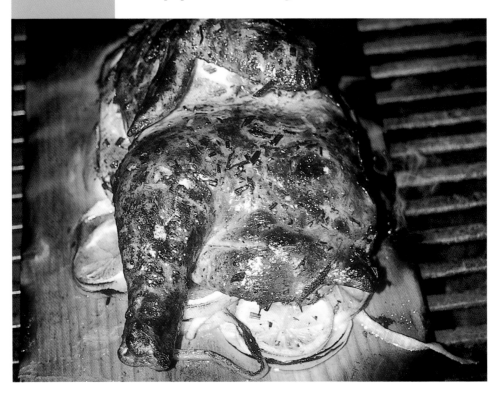

PESTO COUSCOUS-STUFFED CHICKEN BREASTS

- 4 boneless, skinless chicken breasts
- 1/2 cup chicken broth
- 1/3 cup couscous
- 1/3 cup pesto
- Salt and pepper to taste
- 1 plank soaked in water
  (see page 15, "Plank Preparation")

PESTO

- 1/2 cup loosely packed, washed basil leaves
- 1 clove garlic, minced
- 2 teaspoons pine nuts
- 1/4 cup grated parmesan cheese
- 1 tablespoon olive oil

In a small saucepan, bring chicken broth to a boil. Add couscous, cover and remove from heat. Let stand 5 minutes. For pesto, finely chop basil in a food processor or mini-chopper. Add remaining ingredients and blend to form a paste. Stir pesto into couscous mixture, salt and pepper to taste. Butterfly chicken breasts and fill with stuffing. Place on prepared plank. Brush lightly with oil 2-3 times during the cooking process. Grill or bake at 350° 30-35 minutes or until juices run clear.

PREFERRED WOOD:
Alder, oak or cedar.

RECIPE VARIATION:
Bone-in chicken breasts with skin can be substituted, add 5-10 minutes to cooking time. There is no need to brush with oil if the skin is left on.

Poultry

CHEESY SPINACH ROLLS

- 4 boneless, skinless chicken breasts
- 1 cup mozzarella cheese, shredded
- 1 cup spinach, chopped
- 1/3 cup parmesan cheese
- 1/3 cup ricotta or cottage cheese
- 1 teaspoon dried oregano
- Olive oil to drizzle
- Salt and pepper to taste
- 1 plank soaked in water
  (see page 15, "Plank Preparation")

Flatten each chicken breast between two sheets of wax paper to 1/4" thick. In a bowl, mix cheeses, spinach and oregano. Divide the cheese mixture evenly among the flattened chicken breasts. Spread cheese mixture over entire surface of breast leaving 1/2" on one edge to seal roll. Roll up breasts and place seam side down on prepared plank. Drizzle olive oil over each rolled breast. Salt and pepper to taste. Grill or bake at 350° 20-25 minutes or until juices run clear.

PREFERRED WOOD: Oak, alder or hickory.

RECIPE VARIATION: Bone-in chicken breasts with skin can be substituted by butterflying open, add 10-12 minutes to cooking time. There is no need to brush with oil if the skin is left on.

SUMATRAN SATAY

- 1 pound boneless, skinless chicken breasts
- 1/3 cup coconut milk
- 1 tablespoon lime juice
- 1 tablespoon vegetable oil
- 1 tablespoon chile sauce
- 2 teaspoons sugar
- 1 teaspoon soy sauce
- Metal or wooden skewers (soak wooden skewers overnight in water)
- 1 plank soaked in water (see page 15, "Plank Preparation")

PEANUT SAUCE:

- 1/3 cup natural peanut butter
- 1/4 cup coconut milk
- 2 tablespoons soy sauce
- 1 tablespoon rice vinegar
- 1 clove garlic
- 1" ginger root, peeled
- 1/4 teaspoon coriander
- Dash of cayenne pepper

Slice chicken breasts into long, thin strips. In a medium bowl, combine coconut milk, lime juice, hot sauce, sugar and soy sauce. Add chicken strips and marinate in refrigerator 1-3 hours. Combine all ingredients for peanut sauce in a blender or mini-chopper. Blend until smooth, set aside. Thread chicken on skewers. Place on prepared plank. Grill or bake at 350° 15 minutes, turn, cook an additional 10-12 minutes or until chicken is no longer pink. Serve peanut sauce for dipping.

PREFERRED WOOD: Oak, alder or hickory.

RECIPE VARIATION: Chicken can be cut into cubes and cooked kebab style.

5-SPICE CHICKEN

- 4 chicken breasts with bone in
- 1 tablespoon sesame oil
- 1 tablespoon canola oil
- 2" fresh ginger, sliced
- 2 teaspoons minced garlic
- 2 teaspoons Chinese 5 spice
- 2 tablespoons soy sauce
- 1 plank soaked in water
  (see page 15, "Plank Preparation")

Place chicken in a zip-lock bag. Add remaining ingredients. Seal bag and mix by hand. Marinate in refrigerator 1-6 hours. Place chicken breasts skin side up on prepared plank. Grill or bake at 350° 40-50 minutes or until juices run clear.

PREFERRED WOOD: Alder, hickory or oak.

RECIPE VARIATION: This recipe also works well with chicken legs and thighs.

Poultry

CHICKEN WITH PARSLEY

- 1 3- or 4-pound chicken, cut up
- 1 cup plain yogurt
- 1 cup fresh parsley leaves
- 1/4 cup whiskey
- 2 tablespoons lemon juice
- 2 cloves garlic, minced
- 1 teaspoon salt
- 1 plank soaked in water
  (see page 15, "Plank Preparation")

In a medium bowl, combine all ingredients. Marinate at least 3 hours and up to 12. Place chicken pieces skin side up on prepared plank. Grill or bake at 350° 40-50 minutes or until juices run clear.

PREFERRED WOOD: Alder, oak or maple.

RECIPE VARIATION: Substitute cilantro for parsley and white wine for whiskey.

Poultry

SOUTH OF THE BORDER LEGS

(see page 15, "Plank Preparation")

- 1 pound chicken legs
- 1/3 cup canola oil
- 1 tablespoon vinegar
- 1 tablespoon chili powder
- 1 teaspoon ground oregano
- 1 teaspoon salt
- 1-4 dashes hot pepper sauce, optional
- 12 ounces tortilla chips, finely crushed
- 1 plank soaked in tequila or water
  (see page 15, "Plank Preparation")

In a medium bowl, whisk together oil, vinegar and spices, blending well. Add chicken legs and marinate at least 30 minutes. Crush tortilla chips in a zip-lock bag or a food processor. Sprinkle chips in a shallow dish. Coat each chicken leg with chips and place on a prepared plank. Grill or bake at 350° 40-50 minutes or until juices run clear.

PREFERRED WOOD: Alder, cedar or oak.

RECIPE VARIATION: Chicken breasts, thighs or wings can be used in this recipe.

Poultry

Hot & Spicy Buffalo Wings

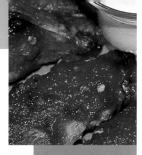

- 2 pounds chicken wings
- 1 8-ounce can tomato sauce
- 2 tablespoons hot sauce
- 1 jalapeño pepper, minced
- 1 tablespoon red pepper flakes
- 1 teaspoon garlic powder
- 1 teaspoon onion powder
- 1 teaspoon white sugar
- Ranch dressing for dipping
- 1 plank soaked in water
  (see page 15, "Plank Preparation")

Cut chicken wings in two at the joints, set aside. In a large bowl, combine all remaining ingredients. Add chicken to sauce and toss until fully coated. Place on prepared plank. Grill or bake at 350° 10 minutes, turn, coat with more sauce, cook 15-20 additional minutes or until juices run clear.

PREFERRED WOOD: Alder, hickory or cedar.

RECIPE VARIATION: For even more fire, add 1 tablespoon diced habanero chilies. Blue cheese dressing also makes a good dipping sauce.

Poultry

SZECHWAN CASHEW CHICKEN

- 2 boneless, skinless chicken breasts, cubed
- 1 tablespoon cornstarch
- 1 tablespoon rice vinegar
- 1 tablespoon soy sauce
- 1 teaspoon chile oil
- 2 tablespoons Hoisin sauce
- 2 tablespoons peanut oil, divided
- 2 teaspoons ginger root, minced
- 2 teaspoons garlic, minced
- 1 red bell pepper, chopped
- 1/2 medium onion, chopped
- 1 8-ounce can bamboo shoots, drained
- 1/2 cup cashews
- 1 plank soaked in water
  (see page 15, "Plank Preparation")

In a medium bowl, combine cornstarch, vinegar, soy sauce, chile oil, 1 tablespoon peanut oil and Hoisin sauce. Add chicken, marinate 20-30 minutes. Heat 1 tablespoon peanut oil in a skillet on high heat, stir-fry cashews 1 minute or until lightly browned. Remove cashews and set aside. Add marinated chicken to skillet, stir-fry 5-7 minutes. Add onion, garlic and ginger and continue cooking until onions are soft. Add red bell pepper, bamboo shoots and browned cashews. Make an edge for the plank using aluminum foil. Once all ingredients are heated throughout, place on prepared plank. Place on direct heat 5-7 minutes or until plank begins to smoke. Serve over a bed of white rice.

PREFERRED WOOD: Alder, hickory or apple.

ITALIAN CHICKEN

- 6 chicken legs or thighs
- 1 cup red wine
- 2 tablespoons olive oil
- 1 tablespoon Italian seasoning
- 1 tablespoon lemon juice
- 1 teaspoon meat tenderizer
- 1 plank soaked in red wine or water
  (see page 15, "Plank Preparation")

Place chicken in a zip-lock bag. Add wine, olive oil, Italian seasoning, lemon juice and tenderizer to the bag. Seal bag and mix by hand. Marinate in the refrigerator 1-6 hours. Place chicken on prepared plank. Grill or bake at 350° 40-50 minutes or until juices run clear.

PREFERRED WOOD: Oak, alder or hickory.

RECIPE VARIATION: Chicken breasts and wings can also be used in this recipe.

Poultry

BEER CAN CHICKEN

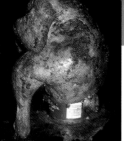

- 1 whole fryer
- 1 can beer
- 3 tablespoons Grill Rub, page 119
- 1 plank soaked in beer or water
  (see page 15, "Plank Preparation")

Remove contents of body cavity from chicken and discard. Rinse chicken thoroughly and pat dry. Rub 1 tablespoon Grill Rub over the outside of the chicken. Sprinkle 1 tablespoon Grill Rub in both body cavities of the chicken. Open the can of beer and discard (or drink) half. Add the remaining tablespoon of Grill Rub to the beer in the can. Hold chicken, neck up, with large body cavity at the bottom. Lower chicken onto beer can so it fits into the cavity. Using the chicken's legs to balance, place the can and chicken on a prepared plank. Grill or bake at 350° 1 to 1 1/4 hours or until meat thermometer reads 180°. Let chicken rest on can at least 10 minutes before removing and carving. Discard any beer left in can.

PREFERRED WOOD: Alder, oak or cedar.

RECIPE VARIATION: Substitute BBQ seasoning of choice in place of Grill Rub.

Chicken Sausage

- 1 pound uncooked chicken sausage of choice
- 1 plank soaked in apple juice or water
  (see page 15, "Plank Preparation")

Sear sausage on a hot grill and place on prepared plank. Grill or bake at 375° 20-25 minutes.

PREFERRED WOOD: Alder, cedar or oak.

Poultry

TASTY TURKEY

- 1 2-pound boneless, skinless turkey breast
- 1/2 cup strong brewed tea
- 1/3 cup soy sauce
- 1 tablespoon honey
- 2 tablespoons olive oil
- 2 cloves garlic, minced
- 1 teaspoon fresh ground black pepper
- 1 teaspoon ground anise
- 1/4 teaspoon ground cloves
- 1 plank soaked in brewed tea or water
  (see page 15, "Plank Preparation")

In a medium bowl, combine all ingredients. Pierce turkey several times with a fork. Marinate turkey, refrigerated, 3-6 hours. Place on prepared plank. Grill or bake at 350° 40-50 minutes or until meat thermometer reaches 170°.

PREFERRED WOOD: Alder, cedar or oak.

RECIPE VARIATION: This marinade also works well with chicken.

CURRIED TURKEY STEAKS

- 1 2-pound boneless, skinless turkey breast
- 1/3 cup Dijon mustard
- 2 tablespoons honey
- 2 tablespoons soy sauce
- 1 tablespoon vegetable oil
- 1 teaspoon curry powder
- 1 plank soaked in water
  (see page 15, "Plank Preparation")

In a medium bowl, mix all marinade ingredients. Cut turkey breast into four equal steaks. Marinate 1-3 hours. Sear steaks on a well-greased hot grill, 1 minute per side. Place on prepared plank. Drizzle breasts with marinade. Grill or bake at 350° 35-40 minutes or until turkey is no longer pink and juices run clear.

PREFERRED WOOD: Alder, cedar or oak.

RECIPE VARIATION: Substitute boneless chicken breasts for turkey.

Poultry

POULTRY & PECAN PASTA

- 1 cup cooked chicken from Herb Roasted Chicken, page 100 or turkey from Tasty Turkey, cubed, page 112
- 1/3 cup extra virgin olive oil
- 2 cloves garlic, minced
- 1/2 cup onion, finely chopped
- 1/2 cup pecans, finely chopped
- 1 tablespoon fresh parsley
- Salt and pepper to taste
- 8 ounces angel hair pasta, cooked
- Parmesan cheese

Heat olive oil in a skillet on medium-high heat. Add garlic and onions, sauté until soft. Add cubed chicken or turkey, heat thoroughly. Remove from heat and toss in pecans and parsley. Salt and pepper to taste. Toss in cooked pasta, serve immediately. Top with parmesan cheese.

RECIPE VARIATION: Any pasta can be substituted for angel hair.

Poultry

Wild Game

TERIYAKI DALL SHEEP ROAST

- 1 3- or 4-pound sheep roast
- 1 tablespoon brown sugar
- 1 teaspoon salt
- 1 teaspoon freshly ground pepper
- 10-15 whole garlic cloves
- 1/3 cup teriyaki sauce
- 1 plank soaked in red wine or water
  (see page 15, "Plank Preparation")
- Meat injecting syringe

Rinse meat and pat dry. In a small bowl, mix sugar, salt and pepper. Rub sugar mixture into roast on all sides. Using a small sharp knife, pierce meat, inserting a clove of garlic into each incision. Place roast in a medium bowl or baking dish. Fill meat injecting syringe with teriyaki sauce. Shoot liquid into roast in several places. Let sit at room temperature 20 minutes or marinate up to 6 hours in refrigerator. Place roast on a prepared plank, cover with foil, tucking ends of foil 1/2" under plank to seal. Grill or bake at 350° 1 3/4 to 2 hours or until meat thermometer reaches 140°-150°. Uncover during the last 15-20 minutes of cooking and bring plank to heavy smoke if desired. Let roast rest at least 10 minutes prior to carving.

PREFERRED WOOD: Cedar, alder or hickory.

RECIPE VARIATION: Substitute any venison or bighorn sheep roast for Dall sheep.

Wild Game

RUBBED ELK STEAKS

- 1 to 1 1/2 pounds elk backstrap
- 1/4 cup olive oil
- 1 prepared plank soaked in red wine or water
  (see page 15, "Plank Preparation")

GRILL RUB
1 teaspoon salt
1 teaspoon celery seed
1/2 teaspoon brown sugar
1/2 teaspoon granulated onion
1/2 teaspoon onion powder
1/4 teaspoon turmeric
1/4 teaspoon chili powder

Rinse meat and pat dry. Slice backstrap 1/4" thick. In a small bowl, mix all dry rub ingredients. Sprinkle grill rub onto both sides of backstrap slices. Let sit 15-20 minutes at room temperature. Dip steaks into olive oil and sear both sides on a well-greased hot grill. Place on prepared plank. Grill or bake at 350° 5-10 minutes or until desired doneness. Serve with Brown Gravy, page 122 and rice if desired.

PREFERRED WOOD: Alder, cedar or oak.

RECIPE VARIATION: Any big-game backstrap can be substituted for elk.

Wild Game

WHITETAIL TENDERLOIN WITH BLUE CHEESE

Wild Game

- 1 venison tenderloin
- 2 tablespoons red wine
- 4-5 cloves garlic, minced
- 1 teaspoon oregano
- 1 tablespoon olive oil
- Salt and pepper to taste
- 1/4 cup blue cheese, crumbled
- 1 plank soaked in water
  (see page 15, "Plank Preparation")

Rinse meat and pat dry. Pierce venison tenderloin with a fork in several places. Place tenderloin in a zip-lock bag. Add wine, garlic, oregano and oil. Seal bag and mix by hand. Marinate in refrigerator 3-12 hours. On a hot, well-greased grill, sear grill marks into tenderloin, about 1 minute per side. Place on a prepared plank. Grill or bake at 375° 15-25 minutes or until desired doneness. Sprinkle crumbled blue cheese on top of the tenderloin for last 5 minutes of cooking. Let sit 5-10 minutes before slicing.

PREFERRED WOOD: Alder, cedar or oak.

RECIPE VARIATION: Substitute elk steaks for tenderloin. For an Asian tenderloin, substitute venison for wild boar in Asian Barbecued Wild Boar, page 124.

BLACKTAIL BACKSTRAP

- 1 pound blacktail backstrap
- 1/3 cup flour
- 1 tablespoon corn meal
- 1 teaspoon Lawry's Seasoning Salt
- 1/2 teaspoon garlic powder
- 2 tablespoons canola oil
- 1 tablespoon red wine
- 1 plank soaked in water
  (see page 15, "Plank Preparation")

Rinse meat and pat dry. Slice backstrap 1/4" thick. In a small bowl, mix flour, corn meal, garlic powder and seasoning salt. In a large skillet, heat canola oil on medium-high heat. Dredge backstrap slices in flour mixture and fry, turning once until lightly browned, about 1 minute per side. Place fried backstrap on prepared plank. Grill 5 minutes, bringing plank to heavy smoke if desired.

PREFERRED WOOD: Alder, cedar or oak.

RECIPE VARIATION: Any venison can be used in this recipe.

Wild Game

MOOSE STEW ON A STICK

- 2 cups moose meat, cubed
- 1/4 cup Mr. Yoshida's Gourmet Sauce
- 1 cup russet potatoes, peeled and cubed
- 1 cup carrots, chopped
- 1 cup celery, chopped
- 1/2 onion, chopped
- Olive or canola oil
- Metal or wooden skewers (soak wooden skewers overnight in water)
- 1 plank soaked in water
  (see page 15, "Plank Preparation")

Place cubed moose meat in a medium bowl. Add gourmet sauce, tossing lightly. Let sit at room temperature 15-20 minutes. Steam or microwave potatoes and carrots until slightly soft, just enough to place easily onto the skewers. Thread skewers, alternating meat and vegetables, leaving one inch on each end. Place skewers on prepared plank. Brush meat and vegetables lightly with oil. Grill or bake at 375° 10-15 minutes. Serve with gravy on the side or poured over the meat and vegetables once removed from skewers.

BROWN GRAVY

- 3 tablespoons butter
- 3 tablespoons flour
- 1 1/2 cups beef broth
- 1 tablespoon Worcestershire sauce
- Salt and pepper to taste

In a medium skillet, melt butter on medium-high heat. Stir in flour and whisk until smooth. Lower heat to medium and slowly add beef broth. Cook 5 minutes at a low boil, continually whisking to avoid lumps. Stir in Worcestershire sauce, add salt and pepper to taste.

PREFERRED WOOD: Alder, cedar or hickory.

RECIPE VARIATION: Any venison can be used in this recipe. Substitute teriyaki or soy sauce for Mr. Yoshida's Gourmet Sauce.

Wild Game

HOT SWISS ANTELOPE STEAK

- 4-6 1" antelope steaks
- 1/2 cup red pepper, chopped
- 1/2 cup green pepper, chopped
- 1/2 cup onion, chopped
- 1 tomato, chopped
- 1-2 jalapeño peppers, chopped
- 2 teaspoons dry mustard
- 1/2 teaspoon salt or meat tenderizer, optional
- Olive oil
- 1 plank soaked in water
  (see page 15, "Plank Preparation")

Sprinkle dry mustard and salt or meat tenderizer over steaks and lightly pound with a meat mallet or tenderizing tool. Brush both sides of steaks with olive oil. In a bowl, mix peppers, onion and tomato. On a hot grill or skillet, sear steaks 30 seconds on each side. Place half of pepper mixture on a prepared plank. Place steaks atop pepper mixture and top with remaining peppers. Grill or bake at 350° 20-25 minutes or until steaks reach desired doneness.

PREFERRED WOOD: Hickory, cedar or alder.

RECIPE VARIATION: Any venison can be substituted for antelope.

Wild Game

ASIAN BARBECUED WILD BOAR

- 1 2-pound wild boar roast
- 1 plank soaked in sake or water
  (see page 15, "Plank Preparation")

5-SPICE RUB

- 1 tablespoon brown sugar
- 1 tablespoon granulated onion
- 1 tablespoon Chinese 5-Spice
- 1 teaspoon garlic salt
- 1/2 teaspoon white pepper

BARBECUE BASTING SAUCE

- 2 tablespoons canola oil
- 1 tablespoon cider vinegar
- 1 tablespoon honey
- 1/2 teaspoon thyme
- 1/2 teaspoon ground allspice
- 1/2 teaspoon smoked paprika

In a small bowl, mix all rub ingredients until thoroughly combined. Wash roast and pat dry. Pierce meat in several places with a fork. Place meat on a plate and massage with rub ingredients. Place in a zip-lock bag and refrigerate at least 8 hours. In a small bowl, mix all basting-sauce ingredients until thoroughly combined. Place meat on a plate and brush on a coating of basting sauce. Let sit at room temperature 15-20 minutes. Place meat on prepared plank, baste again once plank is on the grill. Grill or bake at 350° 1 hour or until meat reaches an internal temperature of 160°. Baste several times throughout the cooking process. Serve with fried rice and hot mustard for dipping.

PREFERRED WOOD: Alder, hickory or cedar.

RECIPE VARIATION: Substitute Wild Boar for pork in Achiote Pork Roast, page 93.

WILD PIGEON WITH PEARS & THYME

- 3-4 pigeons, plucked and dressed
- 1 cup white wine
- 3 tablespoons olive oil
- 5 sprigs fresh thyme
- 1/3 cup fresh parsley
- 1/2 teaspoon salt
- 1/4 teaspoon pepper
- 1 pear, peeled and diced
- 1 zucchini, sliced
- 1 plank soaked in water
  (see page 15, "Plank Preparation")

Soak the plucked, dressed pigeons in lightly salted water 1 hour. Rinse and pat dry. Place pigeon and remaining ingredients, except pear and zucchini, into large zip-lock bag. Marinate 3-6 hours. Drain and discard marinade. Evenly distribute diced pears into body cavity of pigeons. Place sliced zucchini on prepared plank. Place pigeons atop zucchini. Grill or bake at 325° 30-45 minutes. For added smoke flavor use a smoker box. Finish pigeons in a slow-cooker on low heat, cook until tender. Garnish with fresh parsley.

PREFERRED WOOD: Cedar, alder or hickory.

RECIPE VARIATION: Substitute dove, grouse or quail for pigeon.

Wild Game

PHEASANT WITH CILANTRO & YOGURT

Wild Game

- 2 pheasants, fully dressed
- 1 cup plain yogurt
- 1 cup fresh cilantro leaves, coarsely chopped
- 1/4 cup white wine or sherry
- 2 tablespoons canola oil
- 2 tablespoons lime juice
- 2 cloves garlic, minced
- 1 teaspoon salt
- 1/2 bunch fresh cilantro for plank
- 1 plank soaked in water
  (see page 15, "Plank Preparation")

In a medium bowl, combine all ingredients. Marinate birds overnight in refrigerator. Place 1/2 bunch fresh cilantro on prepared plank. Place birds, breast side up, atop cilantro layer. Place cilantro from the marinade on top of pheasant breasts. Cover with foil, tucking ends of foil 1/2" under plank to seal. Remove foil during the last 10-15 minutes of cooking time. Grill or bake at 350° 50-60 minutes or until juices run clear.

PREFERRED WOOD: Alder, oak or hickory.

RECIPE VARIATION: Substitute chukar or Hungarian partridge for pheasant.

Goose In Orange Sauce

- 2 boneless, skinless goose breasts
- 1 tablespoon olive oil
- 1 medium onion, sliced
- 1 orange, peeled and cubed
- 1 cup orange juice
- 1/2 cup chicken broth
- 1 tablespoon red wine vinegar
- 1/4 cup orange marmalade
- 1/2 tablespoon cornstarch
- 1 tablespoon cold water
- 1 plank soaked in water
  (see page 15, "Plank Preparation")

Brush goose breasts with olive oil. On a hot, well-greased grill, sear grill marks into goose breasts, about 1 minute per side. Place goose on prepared plank, cover with foil, tucking ends of foil 1/2" under plank to seal. Grill or bake at 350° 45-60 minutes. Heat olive oil in a medium skillet, add onions sautéing on medium heat until translucent, 5-10 minutes. Add remaining ingredients, except cornstarch and water. Bring ingredients to a boil for 5 minutes. Turn to low and simmer while goose is cooking. Prior to serving goose, mix cornstarch and cold water in a small bowl. Bring orange sauce back to a low boil. Add cornstarch mixture to the orange sauce, stirring constantly. Cook until thickened 3-5 minutes. Cut goose into serving slices and top with orange sauce.

PREFERRED WOOD:
Cedar, hickory or alder.

RECIPE VARIATION:
Substitute duck or wild boar for goose.

PLUM-GLAZED DUCK BREASTS

- 4 boneless, skinless duck breasts
- 2 cups water
- 2 teaspoons salt
- 1 tablespoon canola oil
- 1/2 cup prepared plum sauce, for basting
- 1/2 cup prepared plum sauce, for dipping
- 1 plank soaked in water
  (see page 15, "Plank Preparation")

Soak duck breasts overnight in salted water. Pat dry and brush with olive oil. Brush grill grates lightly with oil. Sear both sides of duck breast, 1-2 minutes per side. Place duck on prepared plank and baste with plum sauce. Grill or bake at 350° 45-60 minutes. Baste with sauce 4-5 times throughout cooking process. Thinly slice and serve with plum sauce for dipping.

PREFERRED WOOD: Cedar, hickory or alder.

RECIPE VARIATION: Cube cooked duck breasts and substitute for elk in Elk with Pasta & Mushrooms, page 132.

Wild Game

TURKEY IN BACON WITH HONEY MUSTARD

- 1 boneless wild turkey breast (approximately 1 pound)
- 2 tablespoons Dijon mustard
- 2 tablespoons rum
- 1 tablespoon honey
- 1 tablespoon canola oil
- 1 teaspoon coriander
- 1/2 teaspoon meat tenderizer, optional
- 3-4 strips of raw bacon
- 1 plank soaked in water
  (see page 15, "Plank Preparation")

Place turkey breast in a zip-lock bag. Add all ingredients, except bacon, to bag. Seal bag and mix by hand. Marinate in refrigerator 1-6 hours. On a hot, well-greased grill, sear grill marks into turkey, about 1-2 minutes per side. Place on a prepared plank. Cover turkey breast with sliced bacon. Grill or bake at 375° 30-45 minutes or until meat thermometer reads 170°.

PREFERRED WOOD: Alder, cedar or hickory.

RECIPE VARIATION: Substitute purchased turkey breast, extending cooking time according to package directions.

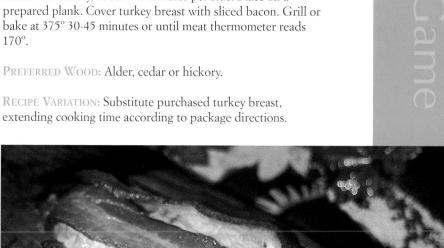

BARBECUED RABBIT

- 1 rabbit, dressed and cut
- 1 onion, chopped
- 2 tablespoons butter
- 1/2 cup cider vinegar
- 1/2 cup ketchup
- 1/4 cup molasses
- 2 tablespoons rum
- 1 teaspoon dry mustard
- Dash of hot pepper sauce, if desired
- 1 plank soaked in water
  (see page 15, "Plank Preparation")

In a medium saucepan, sauté onions in butter over medium heat. When onions are soft, add remaining sauce ingredients. Simmer 10-15 minutes on low heat. Coat rabbit pieces with sauce and place on a prepared plank. Grill or bake at 350° 1 to 1 1/2 hours or until tender. Baste with barbecue sauce often and turn occasionally.

PREFERRED WOOD: Cedar, alder or hickory.

RECIPE VARIATION: Substitute red squirrel, gray squirrel or hare for rabbit.

QUICK & HEARTY STEW

- 2 cups plank-cooked venison or sheep, cubed
- 2 tablespoons butter or bacon grease
- 1 cup onion, chopped
- 2 cloves garlic, minced
- 2 cups potatoes, peeled and cubed
- 1 cup carrots, chopped
- 2 cups beef broth
- 1/2 cup butter
- 1/2 cup flour
- 1 tablespoon Worcestershire sauce
- 3 dried bay leaves
- Salt and pepper to taste

In a large stew pot, melt 2 tablespoons butter on medium-high heat. Add onions and sauté until soft. Add garlic, potatoes and carrots, cover and reduce heat to medium-low. Continue to cook vegetables while preparing the stew base. In a skillet, melt 1/2 cup butter on medium-high heat. Add flour and using a whisk, stir constantly. When mixture is well blended and bubbling, slowly add beef broth, stirring constantly. Permit sauce to reach a boil, reduce heat to low. Add cubed venison or sheep, Worcestershire sauce, bay leaves and salt and pepper to taste. Simmer at least 20 minutes or up to a few hours. Remove bay leaves before serving. If stew becomes too thick, simply add more beef broth or water.

RECIPE VARIATION:
Celery can be added to carrots and potatoes, or vegetables such as bell peppers, spinach or zucchini, can be added with the venison or sheep.

ELK WITH PASTA & MUSHROOMS

- 2 cups plank-cooked elk or deer, cubed
- 8 tablespoons butter
- 1 cup whipping cream
- 3/4 cup parmesan cheese
- 2 tablespoons parsley
- Pepper to taste
- 8 ounces penne pasta, cooked

Melt butter in a heavy skillet, add cream and reduce, stirring constantly until thickened. Add venison, parmesan cheese, pepper and parsley. Simmer 10 minutes. Cook penne pasta to desired tenderness. Toss together and serve.

RECIPE VARIATION: Teriyaki Dall Sheep Roast, page 118 or Plum-Glazed Duck Breasts, page 128, can be substituted for elk or deer.

Wild Game

Desserts

RUM PINEAPPLE

- 1/2 pineapple, peeled and halved
- 1/4 cup rum
- Mint leaves for garnish, if desired
- 1 plank soaked in rum or water
  (see page 15, "Plank Preparation")

This recipe works best with fresh pineapple, but can be made using drained, canned pineapple. Slice pineapple into 1/2-inch segments. Keep pineapple pieces in order for the best presentation on the plank. Place pineapple in a zip-lock bag with the rum. Marinate overnight. Place on prepared plank. Brush the top and sides of the pineapple with canola oil. Grill or bake at 375° 15-20 minutes, or until lightly browned on the edges. Garnish with mint, serve warm or cold.

PREFERRED WOOD: Maple, oak or cherry.

Desserts

APPLE WALNUT TART

- 1 9"-10" prepared pie crust
- 2 apples, peeled, cored and thinly sliced
- 1/2 tablespoon lemon juice
- 1/2 cup walnuts, coarsely chopped
- 1 tablespoon flour
- 3 tablespoons brown sugar
- 1/4 teaspoon cinnamon
- 2 tablespoons butter
- 1 teaspoon cornmeal
- 1 plank soaked in water
  (see page 15, "Plank Preparation")

Place sliced apples in a large mixing bowl, sprinkle with lemon juice. In a small bowl, thoroughly combine walnuts, flour, sugar and cinnamon. Gently toss apples with flour mixture, taking care to completely coat apples. Sprinkle cornmeal evenly over dried plank. Place pie crust over cornmeal. Spread apple-walnut mixture over the pie crust leaving a one-inch edge around the outside. Fold pie crust edges up and over part of the apple-walnut mixture, pinching the crust at even intervals to form the sides. Evenly distribute the butter over the top of the apple-walnut mixture. Grill or bake at 400° 30-35 minutes or until apples are tender and bubbly and crust is browned. If a crispy crust is desired, this can be finished in an oven at 400° on a pizza stone for 5-10 minutes.

PREFERRED WOOD: Apple, maple or oak.

Desserts

CARAMELIZED BANANAS

- 3-4 firm bananas
- 2 tablespoons brown sugar
- 2 tablespoons slivered almonds
- 1 plank soaked in rum or water
  (see page 15, "Plank Preparation")

Peel and slice bananas lengthwise. Place bananas on prepared plank, arrange slightly overlapping. Brush bananas with canola oil. Sprinkle sugar and almonds evenly over bananas. Grill or bake at 350° 15-20 minutes until sugar caramelizes. Serve warm with ice cream.

PREFERRED WOOD: Oak, maple or alder.

Desserts

PEAR CRUNCH

- 2 pears, peeled, cored and thinly sliced
- 1/2 cup white wine
- 1/4 cup flour
- 1/3 cup turbinado sugar
- 1/8 teaspoon nutmeg
- 1 tablespoon oatmeal
- 1/4 cup butter
- 1 plank soaked in water
  (see page 15, "Plank Preparation")

Place sliced pears in a shallow dish. Cover with white wine, set aside. In a small bowl, mix flour, sugar, nutmeg and oatmeal. Using a pastry blender or fork, cut butter into flour mixture until coarsely crumbled. Place pears on prepared plank, arranging slices slightly overlapping, in parallel rows. Top with crunch mixture, taking care to keep the mixture on top of the pears and not on the plank. Grill or bake at 350° 15-25 minutes or until pears are soft and topping is lightly browned.

PREFERRED WOOD: Apple, oak or maple.

Desserts

GINGER PLUM CRUMBLE

- 4-6 firm plums
- 2/3 cup ginger cookie crumbs
- 3 tablespoons butter
- Canola oil
- 1 plank soaked in water
  (see page 15, "Plank Preparation")

Wash, dry and pit plums. Slice thinly, keeping plums together. In a small bowl, cut butter into ginger cookie crumbs using a pastry blender or fork until coarsely crumbled. Place plums on prepared plank, arranging slices slightly overlapping, in parallel rows. Brush sides with canola oil. Top with the crumble mixture, taking care to keep mixture on top of the plums and not on the plank. Grill or bake at 350° 25-35 minutes or until plums are soft and crumble is lightly browned.

PREFERRED WOOD: Maple, oak or apple.

RECIPE VARIATION: Substitute pears for plums.

RHUBARB CRISP

- 4 cups rhubarb, washed and chopped
- 1/2 cup flour
- 1/2 cup sugar
- 1 plank soaked in water
  (see page 15, "Plank Preparation")

TOPPING

- 3 teaspoons crystalized ginger, finely chopped
- 1/3 cup brown sugar
- 1/3 cup white sugar
- 1 cup whole wheat pastry flour
- 1/2 cup butter

In a large bowl, mix rhubarb, flour and sugar. Place mixture into an ovenproof baking dish. Using the same bowl, combine ginger, sugars and flour. Cut butter into flour mixture using a pastry blender or fork until coarsely crumbled. Cover rhubarb with topping mixture. Place baking dish on prepared plank. Grill or bake at 375° 45 minutes or until rhubarb is bubbling and topping is browned.

PREFERRED WOOD: Maple, oak or apple.

Desserts

FRUIT BAKED APPLES

Desserts

- 6 tart apples
- 1 cup loosely-packed brown sugar
- 1/3 cup raisins
- 1/3 cup golden raisins
- 1/3 cup dried cherries
- 1 teaspoon cinnamon
- 5 tablespoons butter, melted
- Canola oil
- 1 plank soaked in apple juice or water
  (see page 15, "Plank Preparation")

Wash and dry apples. Core apples, keeping the bottom of the apple sealed (a grapefruit spoon works well to scoop out the core). In a medium bowl, mix remaining ingredients. Fill apples with sugar and fruit mixture, packing down firmly. Place apples on prepared plank. Brush the outsides of the apple with canola oil. Grill or bake at 375° 20-35 minutes or until apples are soft to the touch. Serve warm with vanilla ice cream or fresh whipped cream.

PREFERRED WOOD: Apple, oak or maple.

GRILLED PEACHES WITH VANILLA TOPPING

- 2-3 peaches
- 1 tablespoon canola oil
- 2 tablespoons molasses
- 1 plank soaked in white wine or water
  (see page 15, "Plank Preparation")

CREAMY VANILLA TOPPING

- 3 tablespoons vanilla yogurt
- 1 1/2 tablespoons sour cream
- Nutmeg

Mix topping and keep refrigerated until ready to serve. Wash and dry peaches. Cut in half and remove pit. Brush entire peach with canola oil. Sear, cut side down, on a preheated grill at medium-high. Cook 2-3 minutes. Lower grill temperature to medium-low. Place peaches, skin side down, on a prepared plank. Drizzle molasses over the peaches. Grill or bake at 350° 30 minutes or until peaches are soft and juicy. Serve warm with topping and a dash of nutmeg.

PREFERRED WOOD: Apple, cherry or maple.

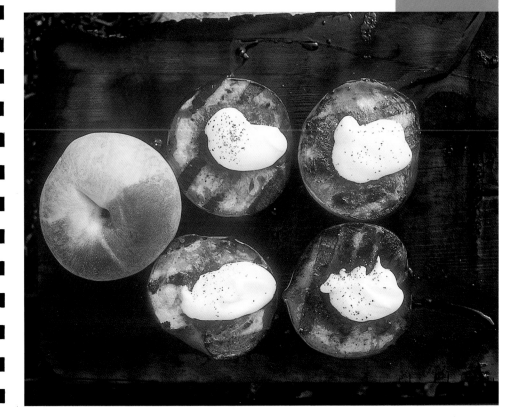

PUMPKIN CUSTARD IN THE SHELL

- 3-4 small pumpkins (1-3 pounds each)
- 6 eggs, beaten
- 2 cups heavy cream
- 3/4 cup brown sugar
- 1/4 cup melted butter at room temperature
- 1 teaspoon vanilla
- 1 1/2 teaspoons cinnamon
- 1/2 teaspoon ginger
- 1/2 teaspoon nutmeg
- 1/4 teaspoon cloves
- Whipped cream, optional
- 1 plank soaked in water
  (see page 15, "Plank Preparation")

Wash and dry pumpkins. Cut off the tops of the pumpkins in a decorative fashion. Scrape all seeds and membrane out of the pumpkin, discard. In a large bowl, mix all remaining ingredients with a wire whisk until well blended. Pour equal amounts of filling mixture into pumpkins leaving at least 1" at the top to allow for expansion. Cover pumpkins with tops and place on prepared plank. Grill or bake at 350° 1 1/2 hours or until filling has set and pumpkins are soft to the touch. Scrape pumpkin away from shell and mix with custard filling, serve warm or chilled right in the pumpkin. Top with whipped cream if desired.

PREFERRED WOOD: Maple, oak or alder.

HOT FUDGE SAUCE

- 1/4 cup butter
- 1/2 cup sugar
- 1/4 cup unsweetened cocoa
- 1/2 cup light cream or half-and-half
- 1/3 cup light corn syrup
- 2 squares unsweetened chocolate
- Dash of salt
- 1 plank soaked in water
- 2 teaspoons vanilla extract
  (see page 15, "Plank Preparation")

Melt butter in a small sauce pan on medium heat. Add remaining ingredients, except for vanilla. Cook, stirring constantly, until sauce comes to a boil and sugar is dissolved. Remove from heat and stir in vanilla. Pour sauce into an ovenproof baking dish. Place on prepared plank. Grill or bake at 350° 10-15 minutes or until sauce begins to bubble.

PREFERRED WOOD: Alder, oak or cedar.

SWEET POTATO CAKE

- 1/2 cup vegetable oil
- 2 large eggs
- 1/2 cup brown sugar
- 1/2 cup white sugar
- 1/4 cup yogurt
- 1 1/2 cups mashed, plank-cooked Apple Baked Sweet Potatoes, page 42, puree
- 2 teaspoons vanilla
- 1 1/4 cups flour
- 1 teaspoon baking powder
- 1/2 teaspoon baking soda
- 2 teaspoons cinnamon
- 1 teaspoon ginger
- 1/2 teaspoon ground nutmeg
- 1/2 teaspoon salt

Preheat oven to 350°. In a large mixing bowl, cream first 7 ingredients. In a medium bowl, mix remaining ingredients until blended. Add dry ingredients to large bowl, mixing until combined. Do not overmix. Bake 45-50 minutes or until cake tests done with a toothpick.

Rob Romig

Recipes

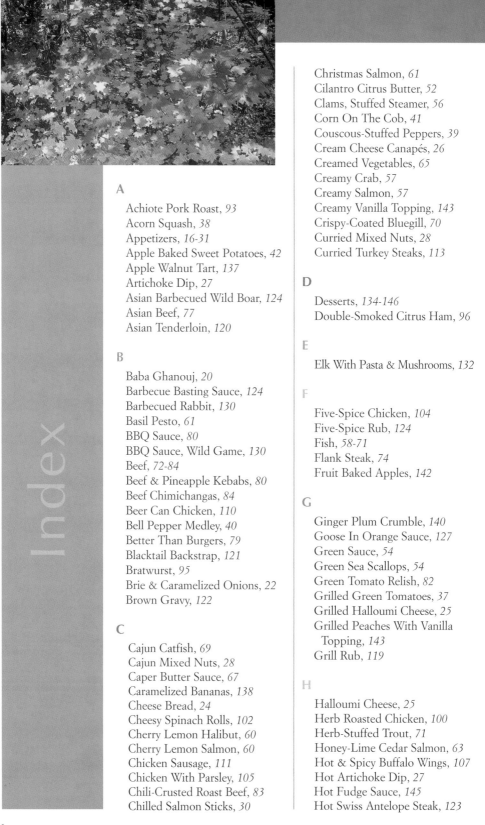

COOKING SALMON & STEELHEAD: EXOTIC RECIPES FROM AROUND THE WORLD

By Scott & Tiffany Haugen

This is not your grandmother's salmon cookbook. The long-time favorites are included and also unique yet easy-to-prepare dishes, like Cabo fish tacos and Tuscan pesto. This cookbook includes: Appetizers, soups & salads, entrees, one-dish meals, exotic tastes, marinades & rubs, outdoor cooking, pastas, stuffed fish, plank cooking, wine selection, scaling and fileting your catch, choosing market fish, cooking tips, and so much more. The Haugens have traveled to and studied cuisines in countries around the world—including the Caribbean, Asia, and Europe—your kitchen is not complete without a copy of *Cooking Salmon & Steelhead*.

Spiral SB: **$24.95**   ISBN: 1-57188-291-X

RECREATIONAL DUNGENESS CRABBING

Scott Haugen

From Alaska to Mexico, Dungeness crabs are pursued for sport and their fine eating quality; *Recreational Dungeness Crabbing* gives you all the information you need to enjoy safe, fun, and productive crabbing. With an emphasis on family, safety, and fun, Haugen covers: natural history of the Dungeness crab; gear; bait; crabbing from a dock or boat; offshore crabbing; raking and dip netting; rod & reel; diving for crabs; crabbing in Oregon and Washington, including hot spots; cleaning and preparing your catch; favorite crab recipes; and more. 6 x 9 inches, 72 pages, full-color.

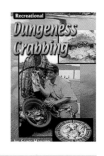

SB: **$12.95**   ISBN: 1-57188-288-X

SUMMER STEELHEAD FISHING TECHNIQUES

Scott Haugen

Scott Haugen is quickly becoming known for his fact-filled, full-color fishing books. This time Haugen explores summer steelhead, including: understanding summer steelhead; reading water; bank, drift, and sight fishing; jigs, plugs, lures, dragging flies, and bait; fishing high, turbid waters; tying your own leaders; egg cures; gathering bait; do-it-yourself sinkers; hatchery and recycling programs; mounting your catch; cleaning and preparation; smoking your catch; and more. With concise text and clear photography, Haugen manages to pack this small book with everything you need to know to enjoy successful summer steelhead fishing. 6 x 9 inches, 136 pages.

SB: **$19.95**   ISBN: 1-57188-295-2

EGG CURES: PROVEN RECIPES & TECHNIQUES

Scott Haugen

Of all the methods anglers can use to catch salmon and steelhead, using natural bait is the most widespread. Of all the natural baits, many consider eggs to be the best. Before this book, you'd have an easier time getting the secret recipe for Coca-Cola than getting a fisherman to part with his personal egg cure. But now, Scott Haugen has done it for you, he went to the experts—fishermen and fishing guides—to get their favorite egg cures and fishing techniques, plus their secret tricks and tips. The result is this book. These 28 recipes come from anglers who catch fish—read this book and you will too. Guaranteed! 5 1/2 x 8 1/2 inches, 90 pages.

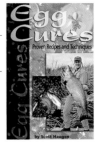

SB: **$15.00**   ISBN: 1-57188-238-3